Programming in QuickBASIC

BOOKS AVAILABLE

By both authors:

BP306 A Concise Introduction to Ami Pro 3
BP327 DOS one step at a time
BP337 A Concise User's Guide to Lotus 1-2-3 for Windows
BP341 MS-DOS explained
BP343 A concise introd'n to Microsoft Works for Windows
BP346 Programming in Visual Basic for Windows
BP351 WordPerfect 6 explained
BP352 Excel 5 explained
BP353 WordPerfect 6.0 for Windows explained
BP354 Word 6 for Windows explained
BP362 Access one step at a time
BP372 CA-SuperCalc for Windows explained
BP387 Windows one step at a time
BP388 Why not personalise your PC
BP399 Windows 95 one step at a time*
BP400 Windows 95 explained*
BP402 MS Office one step at a time
BP405 MS Works for Windows 95 explained
BP406 MS Word 95 explained
BP407 Excel 95 explained
BP408 Access 95 one step at a time
BP409 MS Office 95 one step at a time
BP415 Using Netscape on the Internet
BP419 Using Microsoft Explorer on the Internet
BP420 E-mail on the Internet
BP426 MS-Office 97 explained
BP428 MS-Word 97 explained
BP429 MS-Excel 97 explained
BP430 MS-Access 97 one step at a time

By Noel Kantaris:

BP232 A Concise Introduction to MS-DOS
BP258 Learning to Program in C
BP259 A Concise Introduction to UNIX*
BP261 A Concise Introduction to Lotus 1-2-3
BP264 A Concise Advanced User's Guide to MS-DOS
BP274 A Concise Introduction to SuperCalc 5
BP284 Programming in QuickBASIC
BP325 A Concise User's Guide to Windows 3.1

Programming in QuickBASIC

by

Noel Kantaris

BERNARD BABANI (publishing) LTD.
THE GRAMPIANS
SHEPHERDS BUSH ROAD
LONDON W6 7NF
ENGLAND

PLEASE NOTE

Although every care has been taken with the production of this book to ensure that any projects, designs, modifications and/or programs, etc., contained herewith, operate in a correct and safe manner and also that any components specified are normally available in Great Britain, the Publishers and Author(s) do not accept responsibility in any way for the failure (including fault in design) of any project, design, modification or program to work correctly or to cause damage to any equipment that it may be connected to or used in conjunction with, or in respect of any other damage or injury that may be so caused, nor do the Publishers accept responsibility in any way for the failure to obtain specified components.

Notice is also given that if equipment that is still under warranty is modified in any way or used or connected with home-built equipment then that warranty may be void.

First Published - June 1990
Reprinted - October 1992
Reprinted - April 1994
Reprinted - June 1995
Revised and Reprinted - November 1996
Reprinted - June 1998
Reprinted - July 2000

British Library Cataloguing in Publication Data
Kantaris, Noel
Programming in QuickBASIC
1. IBM, PC. Microcomputer systems.
I. Title
005.265

ISBN 0 85934 229 8

Cover Design by Gregor Arthur
Cover illustration by Adam Willis
Printed and Bound in Great Britain by Cox & Wyman Ltd, Reading

PREFACE

QuickBASIC is one of the two most popular structured and compiled dialects of BASIC in use today on IBM and compatible computers. It comes in the form of a complete package with its own editor, compiler, debugger, etc., and its own user interface.

The original version of BASIC (which stands for Beginner's All-purpose Symbolic Instruction Code) was first developed as a teaching language at Dartmouth College in 1964. In 1978 'standard BASIC' was adopted as a result of recommendations on the minimal requirements on the language. BASICA, written by Microsoft for use with the IBM PCs, and GWBASIC (its equivalent form running on compatibles), is an enhanced version of standard BASIC, embodying nearly 200 commands. These were bundled with pre-DOS 5 versions of the operating system, but users of MS-DOS 5 or higher have access to a cut-down version of Microsoft's QuickBASIC, which we shall call QBASIC to distinguish it from QuickBASIC.

However, all the above versions of BASIC (excluding QuickBASIC), are interpreted languages. This means that each and every statement has to be interpreted by a separate program called the interpreter before execution, each time such statements are encountered, even if it is a thousand times, as in the case of statements appearing within loops.

QuickBASIC, on the other hand, is a compiled language. A separate program, called the compiler is used to check the whole program for errors and then compiles it into the machine specific code that will actually be executed by the computer. Thus, statements within loops are only checked once, which makes a compiled program far more efficient than an interpreted one. A diagrammatical representation of the compiling process is shown overleaf.

QuickBASIC uses a threaded interpreted code - translating each line of the BASIC source program into an intermediate code - known as pseudo-code, which closely resembles machine code. When a program is run the pseudo-code is translated to full machine code and executed. Since, however, the pseudo-code still has connections with the original source code, the user can interact with the program in a manner similar to that provided by traditional interpreters. Thus, QuickBASIC exploits the best of both worlds.

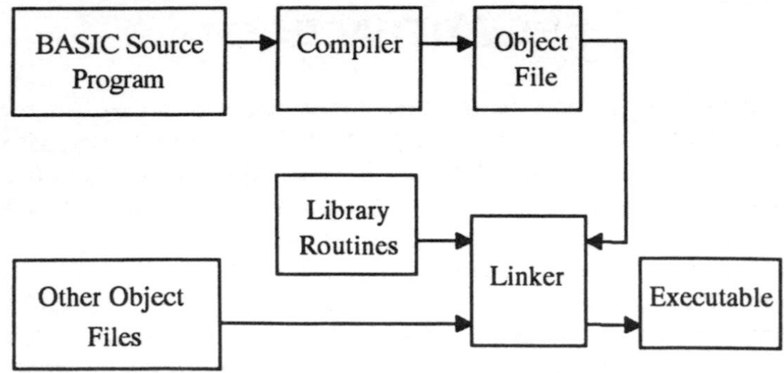

QuickBASIC supports extensive control structures, local variables and parameter passing in procedures and does not require line numbers. Thus, programs can be written in modular form which when compiled provide the building blocks for larger and more complicated applications. Furthermore, it can access the computer's entire memory and is not confined to the 64 kBytes of memory of BASICA or GWBASIC.

QuickBASIC can load and run programs written in Microsoft BASIC, BASICA, aand GWBASIC with minimal changes in statements such as DRAW, PLAY, POKE, and USR, while other statements which apply to program housekeeping such as AUTO, DELETE, EDIT, LIST, LOAD, MERGE, MOTOR, NEW, OPEN, RENUM and SAVE cannot be used.

Users of QBASIC can exploit all the structure benefits of QuickBASIC, but cannot produce a compiled version of their program.

ABOUT THIS BOOK

This book is a guide to programming using QuickBASIC and QBASIC (the free version that comes with the operating system for MS-DOS 5 or higher users. The reader is not expected to have any familiarity with the language as statements are introduced and explained with the help of simple programs. The user is encouraged to type these into the computer, save them, and keep improving them as more complex language statements and commands are encountered. Graded problems are set throughout the book, with full working solutions appearing at the back of the book. At the end of each Chapter, additional graded exercises are presented, some with financial or scientific bent, so that users have a choice in both the level of problem difficulty and the field of application.

Chapters 1-3 deal with the basic QuickBASIC statements which control program flow and allow the user to manage with most aspects of the language. Chapters 4-5 introduce the concepts of strings, arrays and subprograms which expand the programming capabilities of the user beyond the beginner's level. Chapter 6 deals entirely with disc file handling techniques and should be of special interest to those who need to process large quantities of data. Three types of data files are discussed, namely, sequential, random and binary types. A general program that can create and retrieve any random file is discussed in Appendix C. The program can become the basis of database design.

If you would like to purchase a floppy disc containing all the files/programs that appear in this, or any other listed book(s) by the same author(s), then fill in the form at the back of the book and send it to the stipulated address.

ABOUT THE AUTHOR

Graduated in Electrical Engineering at Bristol University and after spending three years in the Electronics Industry in London, took up a Tutorship in Physics at the University of Queensland. Research interests in Ionospheric Physics, led to the degrees of M.E. in Electronics and Ph.D. in Physics. On return to the UK, he took up a Post-Doctoral Research Fellowship in Radio Physics at the University of Leicester, and in 1973 a Senior Lectureship in Engineering at The Camborne School of Mines, Cornwall, where since 1978 he has also assumed the responsibility of Head of Computing.

ACKNOWLEDGEMENTS

I would like to thank colleagues at the Camborne School of Mines for the helpful tips and suggestions which assisted me in the writing of this book. In particular, I would like to thank Andrew Torry for implementing the program of Appendix C.

TRADEMARKS

BASICA, GW-BASIC, QBASIC, QuickBASIC and **MS-DOS** are registered trademarks of Microsoft Corporation

IBM and **PC-DOS** are registered trademarks of International Business Machines Corporation

CONTENTS

1. PACKAGE OVERVIEW

It is assumed here that you have followed the instructions accompanying the software, relating to its installation on the hard disc of your computer, or its use from a floppy drive. If you are using an already installed package on hard disc, then it is most likely that the files which make up the complete package will be found in a subdirectory of your computer's hard disc, and that the actual program can be invoked by typing **QBasic** or **QB** at the root directory's prompt. An appropriately written batch file would then locate the subdirectory in which the program's files reside and load the **QB.EXE** file (the front-end user interface of the package) into memory.

If you are about to install the package on your hard disc for the first time, then log onto the A: drive, run the SETUP program on Disc #1, and choose the full installation option, specifying the following directory structure.

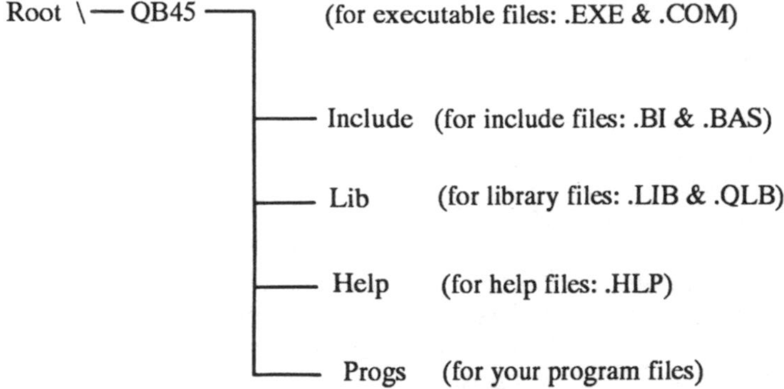

Then choose to install the package under the above configuration. While the program is installing the package, you will be told that two additional directories are needed for the installation of the 'example' and 'advisory' files, and you will be asked whether these should be set up. Agree with this suggestion by pressing the <Enter> key.

You will now need to write two batch files, one to set up the correct environment for QuickBASIC - call it **qbasic.bat**, and the other to free and restore the environment to its original state when you exit from the package - call it **quit.bat**.

Assuming that all your batch files are to be found in a subdirectory called BATCH, and all the DOS files in the subdirectory called DOS, then these two batch files could take the form shown below (if your DOS version is below 3.3, then omit the @ sign which precedes the echo command in the batch files).

The **qbasic.bat** file could contain the commands:

```
@echo off
cls
cd c:\qb45\progs
path=c:\;c:\dos;\c:\batch;c:\qb45
set include=c:\qb45\include
set lib=c:\qb45\lib
set help=c:\qb45\help
```

The **quit.bat** file could contain the commands:

```
@echo off
cls
cd\
set include=
set lib=
set help=
path=c:\;c:\dos;\c:\batch
```

If your system is correctly implemented, typing **qbasic** at the C:\> prompt, executes the appropriate batch file which sets the correct environment and puts you into the C:\QB45\PROGS subdirectory. Now typing **qb**, causes the QuickBASIC opening screen, containing the Copyright message, to be displayed on your screen.

You could, of course, include the **qb** command at the end of the **qbasic.bat** file, and also append the commands within the **quit.bat** file to it, so that the one batch file does the complete job. Whichever method you choose, when you activate QuickBASIC, nine items appear on the top of the screen, called the main menu, as shown on the next page.

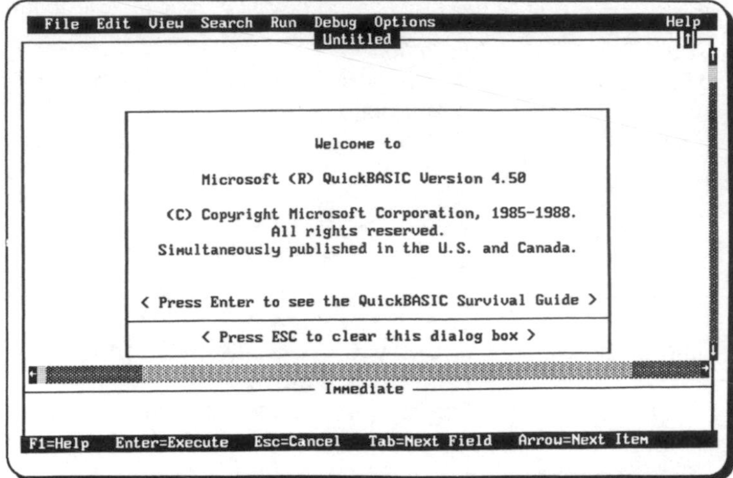

At this point, you can either press <Enter> to be guided through the 'Survival Guide', or <Esc> to clear the screen and enter the 'editor'.

The QuickBASIC Edit Screen:

The edit screen is subdivided into several areas as shown below.

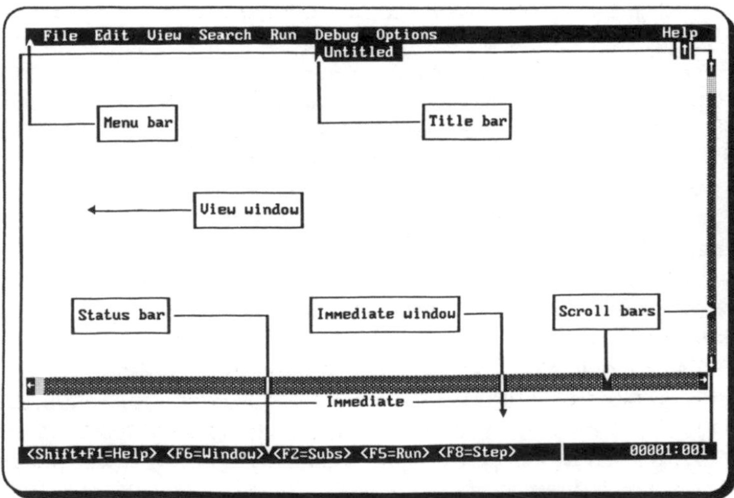

The various areas of the edit screen have the following function:

Area	*Function*
Menu bar	Allows you to choose from several main menu options
Title bar	Displays the name of the current program. If a new program, it displays the word <Untitled>
View window	Allows you to enter a new program or load and view an old program
Scroll bars	Allows you to scroll the screen with the use of the mouse
Immediate window	Allows you to execute BASIC commands in immediate mode
Status bar	Displays the current program status and information on the present process.

The Main Menu

Each main menu option has associated with it a pull-down sub-menu. To activate the main menu, either press the <Alt> key, which causes the first item of the menu (**F**ile) to be highlighted, then use the right and left arrow keys to highlight any of the items in the main menu, or use the mouse to point to an item. Pressing either the <Enter> key, or the left mouse button, reveals the pull-down sub-menu of the highlighted menu item.

Main menu options can also be activated directly by pressing the <Alt> key followed by the first letter of the required option. Thus pressing **Alt+O**, causes the pull-down sub-menu of the 'Options' to be displayed. You can use the up and down arrow keys to move the highlighted bar up and down a sub-menu, or the right and left arrow keys to move along the options of the main menu. As each option is highlighted, a short description of the function of the relevant option or command appears in the status line. Pressing the <Enter> key selects the highlighted option or executes the highlighted command. Pressing the <Esc> key closes the menu system and returns you to the editor.

Before going on, activate the 'Options' menu and highlight and select the 'Full menu' option so that full sub-menus are displayed when each of the main menu items are chosen. If you don't do this at this point, what is described below might not be what is displayed on your screen.

The Main Menu Options:

The DOS 5 QBASIC version has much shorter menus than the ones shown here, which are those of the full QuickBASIC package. Each item of the main menu offers the options:

File:

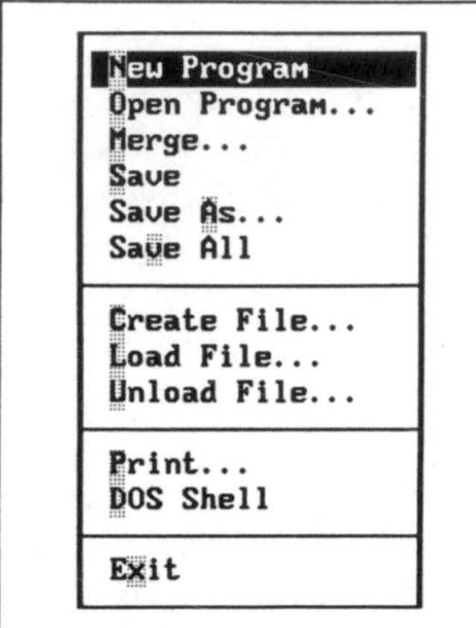

Produces a pull-down menu, as shown, of mainly file related tasks, such as loading or saving a program, printing text or program listings, interact with DOS and exit the package. You can select such options or execute such commands by pressing the shaded letter in the sub-menu. On colour displays, the shaded letters appear emboldened and in different colour to the rest of the text.

Edit:

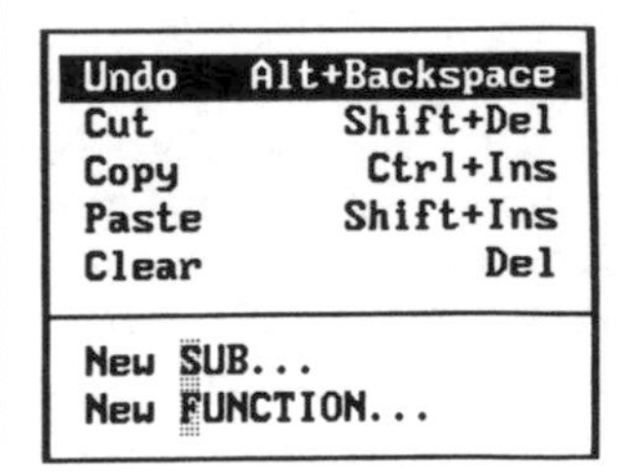

Used to cut, copy and paste text or create user defined subprograms and functions. Marked text (use the <Shift> key with arrow keys from within the editor) can be cut out and pasted on to another part of the display. The Clear option deletes a marked block completely.

View:

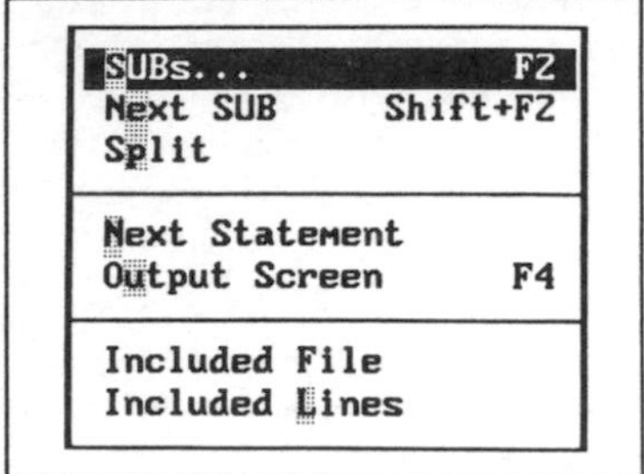

Used to view selected text and output. Subprograms and functions are listed in alphabetical order and in order of module. The Split option allows two modules, or two different areas of a program, to be displayed simultaneously on screen. The Included options allow contents of included files to be seen.

Search:

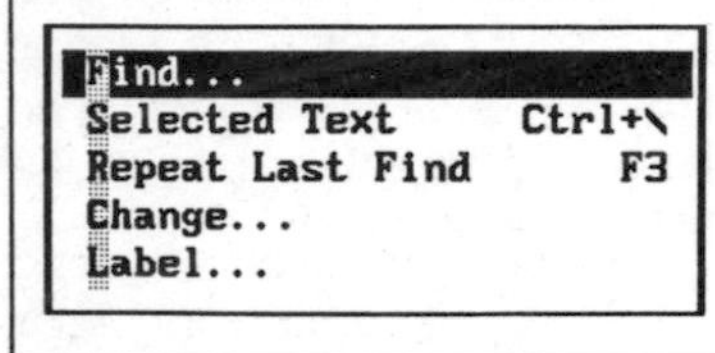

Used to find and replace specific text. The Change option can be used to give variables a new name. The Label option searches for specific labels or references to labels.

Run:

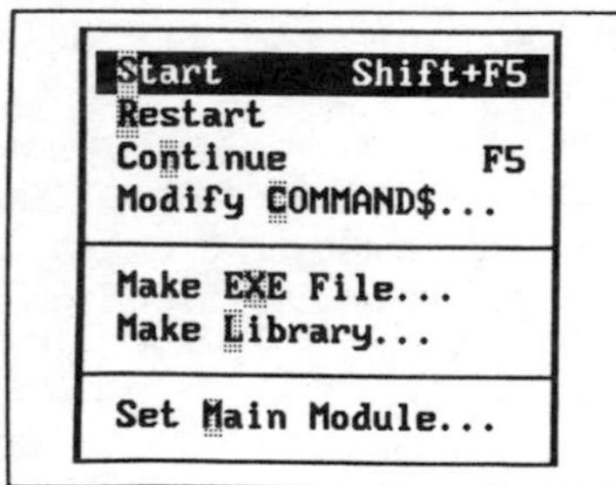

Used to execute a program, continue execution of an interrupted program, create executable (.EXE) files, or turn subprograms and functions into library routines, with the use of Make Library option, for use with other programs. The COMMAND$ option allows access to parameters which are specified in a DOS command line.

Debug:

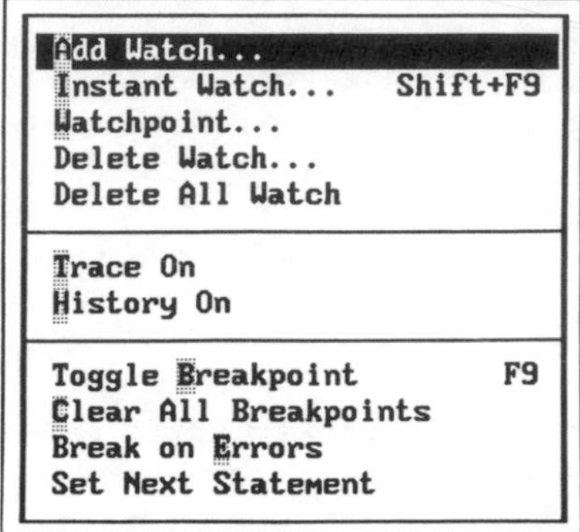

Used to debug a program. The Watch option allows you to monitor the value taken by certain variables during program execution. Use the Toggle Breakpoint option to set the break point within the program. The Trace On option allows you to trace the progress of a program, while the History option allows you to backtrack through the last 20 statements prior to the one that caused the error.

Calls:

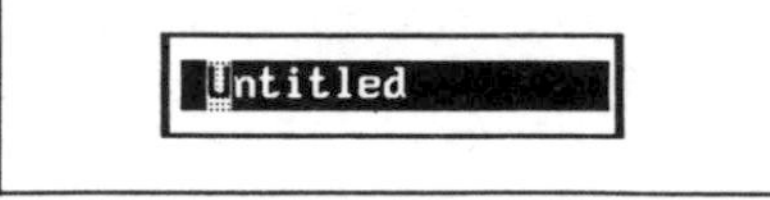

Used to display active subprograms or functions. It displays a list of the last 5 subprogram calls (the most recent one being on the top of the list). This menu option is not available in the DOS version of QuickBASIC.

Options:

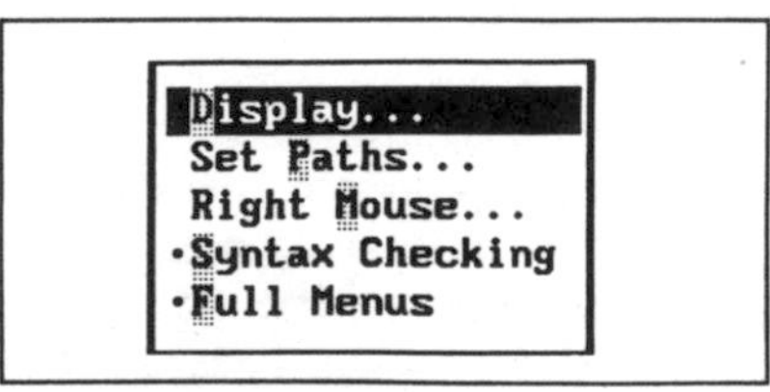

Used to configure the display screen and the right mouse button, set directory paths, or choose between displaying full and short pull-down menus. The Syntax Checking option warns of errors when a program line is entered.

Help:

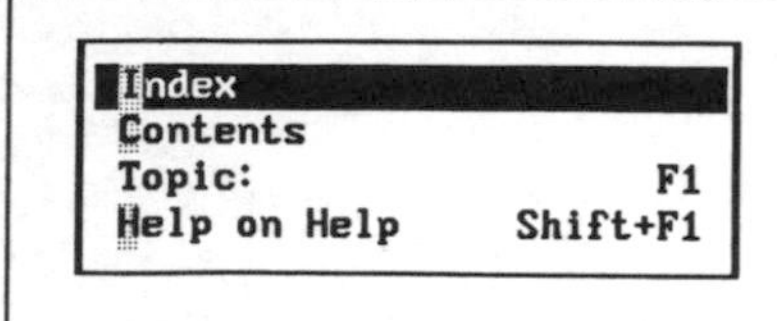

Used to display the help index, help on specific topics, and help on help. Context-sensitive help can can also be activated on request (see below).

Help Screens:
QuickBASIC has context-sensitive help screens which explain the use of the items in the various menus or commands from within a program. Thus, to obtain help information on the use of the options offered under **File**, first choose the **File** option of the main menu, then use the arrow keys to highlight the desired task from the pull-down menu, and press the **F1** function key.

Dialogue Boxes:
Three periods after a sub-menu option or command, means that a dialogue box will open when the option or command is selected. A dialogue box is used for the insertion of additional information, such as the name of a file to be loaded, or to be acted upon in some way.

To understand dialogue boxes, type the word 'hi' in the edit screen, then press **Alt+S**, and select the **C**hange option from the revealed sub-menu. The dialogue box shown on the next page will now appear on the screen.

When a dialogue box opens, the <Tab> key can be used to move the cursor from one field to another, while the <Enter> key is used only to indicate that the options within the various fields within the dialogue box are specified correctly. Every dialogue box contains one field which is enclosed in emboldened angle-brackets (<Find and Verify>, shaded in the above example). This field indicates the action that QuickBASIC will take if the <Enter> key is pressed (in our example, the word 'hi' will be changed to 'hello', if this is what we choose to type against the 'Find What' and 'Change To' fields. Pressing the <Esc> key aborts the menu option and returns you to the editor.

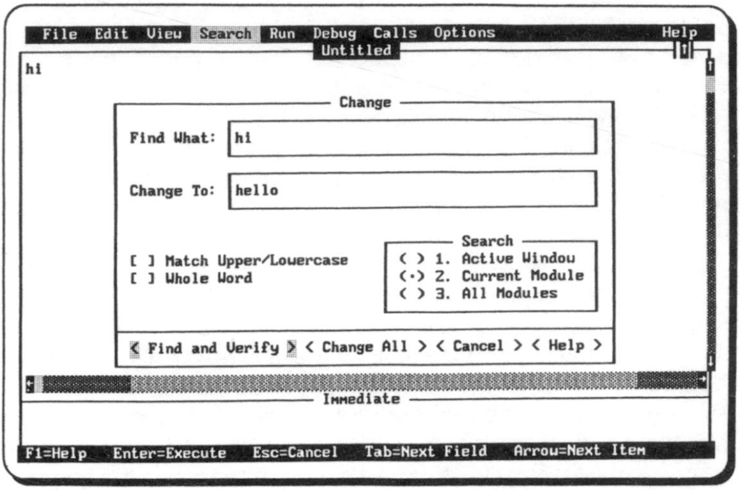

```
 File  Edit  View  Search  Run  Debug  Calls  Options                    Help
                               Untitled
hi

                        ─────────── Change ───────────
      Find What:  hi

      Change To:  hello

                                              ─── Search ───
      [ ] Match Upper/Lowercase              ( ) 1. Active Window
      [ ] Whole Word                         (•) 2. Current Module
                                             ( ) 3. All Modules

      < Find and Verify > < Change All > < Cancel > < Help >

                               Immediate

F1=Help   Enter=Execute   Esc=Cancel   Tab=Next Field   Arrow=Next Item
```

Using the Windows:

When the QuickBASIC package is loaded, there are two active windows on the screen. The largest one is the 'view' window used by the editor and the other is the 'immediate' window at the bottom of the screen where BASIC instructions can be typed for processing in the immediate mode. For example, you can type ?x (which stands for print the value of x) if you want to see what is held in the variable x after a program is run.

QuickBASIC activates a third window at the top of the screen (called the 'watch' window) when you use certain debug commands, to monitor the value taken by certain variables during program execution.

You can move from the view window to the immediate window, and back by pressing the **F6** function key. The window which the cursor is in, is referred to as the 'active' window. An active window can be enlarged or reduced by using the mouse to drag the partitioning line to its desired position.

The active window can further be toggled between filling the entire screen or returning it to its former size by pressing **Ctrl+F10** alternately. Pressing **Ctrl+F10** once, expands the active window, while pressing **Ctrl+F10** again, reduces it.

Splitting the View Window:
Sometimes it might be necessary to view different parts of a program simultaneously. If the program is so large that it can not be viewed on the screen without scrolling, then you might consider splitting the screen horizontally into two portions. This can be done by pressing **Alt+V**, and selecting the **S**plit option from the sub-menu. Selecting **S**plit a second time restores the view window to its single-window configuration.

Splitting the view window does not allow you to load a separate program in each window. You are always working with the same program, but viewing separate parts of it. The part of the window that the cursor is in is the active window. To move the cursor to the next window simply press the **F6** function key. You can use a split window configuration to cut and paste information from one window to the other, view the main program in one and a subprogram in the other, or view one part of a program while editing another part of the same program.

The Editor

You can enter a new QuickBASIC program in your computer with the use of either the package's own editor, or a word processor, provided it is of a type that creates an ASCII file and you terminate each program line by pressing the <Enter> key. Choosing the latter option is only worth while if you intend to write long and complicated programs and you are averse to learning all the different commands of yet another editor.

As the programs which will be developed in this book are rather short in length, it is suggested that you use the package's editor to enter them into the computer's memory, remembering that the cursor can be moved to any part of a program and corrections can be made with the use of the key strokes described below:

Key	*Function*
Left arrow	moves the cursor to the left by one character
Right Arrow	moves the cursor to the right by one character
Ctrl+Left	moves the cursor to the beginning of the previous word on the current line
Ctrl+Right	moves the cursor to the beginning of the next word on the current line
Home	moves the cursor to the first column of the current line

End	move the cursor to the end of the last word on the current line
Up arrow	moves the cursor up one line
Down arrow	moves the cursor down one line
Ctrl+Home	moves the cursor to the first line of the current screen
Ctrl+End	moves the cursor to the last line of the current screen
PgUp	moves the cursor to the previous screen
PgDn	moves the cursor to the next screen
Ctrl+PgUp	moves the cursor left one screen
Ctrl+PgDn	moves the cursor right one screen
Ins	toggles the Insert mode from ON (its default position) to OFF and back again
Enter	moves the cursor to the beginning of the next line, provided the insert mode is in the ON position
Ctrl+Y	deletes the line at the current cursor position
Ctrl+N	inserts a blank line at the current cursor position
Shift+arrows	marks block areas on the screen to be used with the sub-menu of the **E**dit option, namely **C**ut, **C**opy, **P**ast, and **C**lear.

There are a lot more commands associated with the package's editor, but you'll find that those given above are sufficient for almost all your needs.

When areas of text are marked, with either the use of the Shift+arrows or a mouse, QuickBASIC keeps the contents of a blocked area in a temporary storage area known as the 'clipboard' from which it can be retrieved later when the **C**ut, **C**opy, and **P**aste options are used. The clipboard stores only one block of information at a time; attempting to store a second block, simply overrides the previously stored block.

If you are not using a mouse, you might want to clear the scroll bars from the screen, to give you more room. This can be done by pressing **Alt+O**, selecting the **D**isplay option and pressing the <Tab> key until the cursor is positioned in the 'Scroll Bars' field. Pressing the spacebar toggles the option into the off position by clearing the letter X from within the square brackets.

If you are using a mouse, scrolling text in the view window is easy. Place the mouse pointer on the top, bottom, left or right of the scroll bars and click the left mouse button to scroll upwards, downwards, to the left or to the right, respectively.

Basic Statements

With what was discussed previously in mind, activate QuickBASIC and turn the 'syntax checking' option on (type **Alt+O** to display the 'Options' sub-menu and press **S**). This ensures that every entered line is checked for errors, with minor errors corrected automatically, then use the editor to type and create the following source file which is a program to calculate the average of three numbers.

```
REM Calculate Averages
INPUT "Enter three numbers ",A,B,C
Sum=A+B+C
Average=Sum/3
PRINT "Average value is ";Average
END
```

The above is presented to give you an idea of a QuickBASIC source program. All the statements within it will be discussed in detail in this and following pages. So there is no need to worry!

The REM Statement:

A QuickBASIC source program consists of statements and REM (remark) lines. The program above has one remark line and five statement lines and unlike other BASICs, QuickBASIC does not require line numbers. REM lines, which have no effect on the running of a program, allow the insertion of remarks to help the user to remember the function of program sections.

The INPUT Statement:

The INPUT statement (the second executable statement of the program on the previous page) provides one way of giving variables (see below for definition) a value. In the example, the INPUT statement is written with a string within full quotes ("), so that the user is prompted by the computer on what is expected by the program. Input is provided from the standard input device which in this case is the terminal keyboard.

The values for the variables A, B and C can be entered in any convenient free format - with commas or spaces between the numbers, followed by pressing <Enter>. QuickBASIC provides for a far greater flexibility in data input and output which indeed is one of the strengths of the language, but these will not be discussed at this point as they might confuse the newcomer to the language.

Once variables have values, they can be used in assignment statements and/or expressions in the rest of the program to perform desired calculations. A variable must have a value before it is used in an expression or in the right hand side of an assignment statement.

The PRINT Statement:

The PRINT statement (the penultimate statement in our example program) allows the printing of the result of our calculation. This result is held in the variable named Average. As with the INPUT statement, a string within full quotes follows the word PRINT which allows us to explain what is printed out. The statement PRINT causes output to be sent to the standard output device which is the video display unit (VDU) or screen.

Again, we can delay discussion on formatting the printed output. However, the penalty is that we have to accept the default QuickBASIC form of printing without any control on the number of digits printed out.

The END Statement:

It has been assumed throughout the foregoing discussion that program execution is sequential. The END statement halts execution of the program and can be placed in any part of the program.

Variables and Constants

Variables:

A variable is a quantity that is referred to by name, such as A, B, C, Sum and Average in the previous program. Variables can take on many values during program execution, but you must make sure that they are given an initial value, as QuickBASIC automatically zeros variables initially.

Constants:
A constant is a quantity that either appears as a number (3 in the third executable statement in the previous program) or is referred to by name, but has only one value during program execution; that which was allocated to it by the user.

Expressions:
An expression, when referred to in this text, implies a constant, a variable or a combination of either or both, separated by arithmetic operators.

Naming Convention:
Variable names and constant names are formed by combining upper and lower case letters with numbers (alphanumeric characters only), provided the first character is a letter. The length of the name does not matter, but it must be continuous and not contain a space. The underscore character can be used to make a variable name more meaningful (for example, Average_value). In general, when naming variables, you must be careful not to use a name which is the same as a BASIC reserved word such as

COLOR DRAW INPUT LOOP PRINT RUN SAVE WRITE

to mention but a few. A full list of all QuickBASIC reserved words is given in Appendix A. Reserved words appear in uppercase letters throughout this book, to match the way QuickBASIC converts all reserved words to uppercase, even though you might have typed them in lowercase. Typing PRINT, Print or print has the same meaning to QuickBASIC and will be converted automatically by the compiler to upper case.

There are a variety of *types* for both variables and constants; the most commonly used being the 'integer' and 'floating-point' (otherwise referred to as real) types. An integer type can hold only integer quantities and is distinguished from a floating-point type which holds numbers containing fractional parts. The computer stores these two types differently and tends to calculate much faster when using integer-value variables or constants.

Examples of integer and floating-point numbers are as follows:

-255	is an integer number
26.75	is a real or floating point number
-.45E+16	is an exponential number. The E stands for 'times ten to the power of'.

Less commonly used types of variables and constants are 'long integers' and 'double precision floating point'. In QuickBASIC, the values of single-precision variables are accurate to 6 significant figures, while those of double-precision variables are accurate to 16. String variables can be as long as 32767 characters. However, the combined length of all strings stored in memory at one time must not exceed 65636 characters. These are specified by appropriate tags, as follows:

Name	*Tag*	*Range*	*Variable Type*
Variable_name%	%	-32768 to +32767	Integer
Variable_name&	&	-2147483648 to +2147483647	Long Integer
Variable_name or Variable_name!	!	$\pm 3.4 x 10^{-37}$ to $\pm 3.4 x 10^{+38}$	Single-precision floating-point
Variable_name#	#	$\pm 1.8 x 10^{-307}$ to $\pm 1.8 x 10^{+308}$	Double-precision floating-point
Variable_name$	$		String.

String Variables:

A sequence of characters is referred to as a literal, and a literal in quotation marks is called a string. For example, ABC123 is a literal, and "ABC123" is a string.

Like numbers, strings can be assigned to variables. They are distinguished from numeric variables by a $ after the name, for example A$. A string can be assigned to a string variable by writing A$="ABC123", or through either the INPUT or READ statements (more about this later).

Variable Type Declarations:

Variable types can be declared with the use of the DEFtype statement rather than using type-declaration tags. The various DEFtype declaration statements are as follows:

DEFtype	*Type of Variable*
DEFINT Variable_name	Integer
DEFLNG Variable_name	Long integer
DEFSNG Variable_name	Single-precision floating-point
DEFDBL Variable_name	Double-precision floating-point
DEFSTR Variable_name	String.

Named variables cannot be defined with the DEF statement; what can be defined are all variables *starting* with the letter specified within the DEF statement. More than one such variable can be defined by separating their starting letter with a comma within the DEF statement, while ranges of variables are entered with a hyphen in between their starting letter.

For example, to define all variables starting with letters within the range from I to N, use

```
DEFINT I-N
```

If a floating-point operand is assigned to an integer operand, the floating-point number is first rounded and then truncated to an integer, i.e. assuming that both I and K have been declared as integers (by the statement DEFINT I,K), the statements I=3.5 and K=0.37 will cause QuickBASIC to assign the integer values of 4 and 0 to the constants I and K, respectively. For this precise reason, mixing floating-point constants or variables with integers in arithmetic operations, can have unexpected results! Thus, mixed mode arithmetic is best avoided.

Arithmetic Operators & Priority

We shall now examine how the various arithmetic operations in our first program are performed. The calculations in the program are performed by the third and fourth statements, namely

```
Sum=A+B+C
Average=Sum/3
```

Combining them into one line, we could write

Average=(A+B+C)/3 (**Not** Average=A+B+C/3)

It is important that the numerator of this expression is in brackets. If it were not, BASIC would evaluate first C/3 and then add to it A+B, which would give the wrong result. This is due to an inbuilt system of priorities as shown in the table below:

Arithmetic Operators and their Priority

Symbol	*Example*	*Priority*	*Function*
( )	(A+B)/N	1	Parenthesized operation
^	A^N	2	Raise A to the Nth power
*	A*N	3	Multiplication
/	A/N	3	Division
+	A+N	4	Addition
–	A–N	4	Subtraction

Additional Operators:
There are two operators which are useful when performing integer division. These are \ and the MOD. The \ operator gives the whole number part of the result of a division, while the MOD operator gives the remainder (test these in the immediate window). For example, the program statement

```
PRINT 10\3
```

gives the result 3, while the program statement

```
PRINT 10 MOD 3
```

gives the result 1.

It must be stressed, however, that the numbers on which integer division (\) and MOD operate (called the operands) are first rounded up or down and then converted to integers. Thus, the statements

```
PRINT 10.1\3.1
PRINT 10.1 MOD 3.1
```

will give the same result as before, namely 3 and 1, while

```
PRINT 10.9\3.9
PRINT 10.9 MOD 3.9
```

will give the result of 2 and 3, respectively.

BASIC evaluates expressions, in the order of priority indicated in the table above. Expressions in parentheses are evaluated first; Nested groups in parentheses are evaluated beginning with the innermost grouping and working outwards.

Normally, BASIC cannot accept two consecutive operators, for example A*/N. Others, such as A*-N although legal, is better written as A*(-N). Through the use of parentheses, the order of priority of execution and, therefore, the final value of an expression, can be changed. If a line has an expression which contains several operators of equal priority, BASIC will evaluate it from left to right.

Let us examine how a complicated expression such as

```
Y =(A+B*X)^2/C-D*X^3
```

is evaluated. We assume that A, B, C, D and X have values.

First the parenthesized portion of the expression will be evaluated. Within these parentheses the multiplication has a higher priority and therefore it will be evaluated first. Then, A will be added to it, resulting in a numerical value to which we will assign the letter Z. Now the expression is reduced to the following:

```
Y=Z^2/C-D*X^3
```

The above has two exponential expressions, the leftmost of which is evaluated first. Writing Z1 for the result of Z^2 and X1 for the result of X^3, the expression is now reduced to

```
Y=Z1/C-D*X1
```

Again, since division and multiplication have the same priority, the leftmost expression is evaluated first. Finally, the result of the multiplication is taken away from the result of the division and assigned to Y.

All this procedure is carried out automatically by BASIC, but if you intend to use complicated mathematical expressions you must be familiar with it.

The Assignment Statement:

Note that what appears as an equation above is, in fact, an assignment statement and not an algebraic identity. As long as the values of variables on the right of an equals sign are known, the calculated result will be assigned to the variable on the left of the equals sign.

As an example, consider the following lines:

```
K=0
K=K+1
PRINT K
END
```

where the second line would be meaningless had it been an algebraic expression. In computing terms the statement means 'take the present value in K, add one to it and store the result in K'. When this line is executed, the value of K (set in the first line) is zero and adding one to it results in a new value of K equal to one. On running this program, BASIC will print

```
1
```

on the screen.

Entering & Running a Program

You can enter a program into the computer's memory by using the editor to type it in directly or by loading it from disc. If you happened to have saved the Averages program already, use the **F**ile, **O**pen (or **N**ew) option and specify the full drive/path, if different from the default one which was specified during configuration. Then, use the cursor keys to highlight the name of the file you wish to load and press <Enter>. If you have not saved it previously, then type in the following few lines:

```
REM Calculate Averages
INPUT "Enter three numbers ",A,B,C
Sum=A+B+C
Average=Sum/3
Print "Average value is ";Average
END
```

When you attempt to run a program, the QuickBASIC compiler translates your program (source file) to the machine code that will actually be executed by the computer. The compiled file may or may not be executed immediately; it largely depends on whether you selected from the **R**un menu the **S**tart or the **EX**E file option (with QBASIC that comes with DOS 5, you cannot compile a program and the **EX**E option is not available to you. In the full package, the first choice compiles and executes the program, while the second choice only compiles the program producing an executable file.

In either case, if there are any compilation errors, an appropriate error message will appear on the view window and the compiler will inform you which line in your source file is in error. In such a case, edit the original source file and rerun the program. This can be achieved directly by pressing **Alt+R** followed by <Enter>, or by simply pressing the **F5** function key. If there are no compilation or linking errors, execution of the program will start immediately, first by clearing the screen, and then by prompting you for input, as follows:

```
Enter three numbers _
```

Note the cursor waiting for input. This will be the case with this particular program because we used the INPUT statement at the very beginning of the program and the computer is waiting for input. Typing

```
2,3,5
```

the three numbers separated by commas, corresponding to variables A, B and C in the INPUT statement of the program, causes the computer to respond with

```
Average value is 3.333333
```

when the <Enter> key is pressed.

Pressing any key, returns you to the view window of the QuickBASIC environment.

Saving a Program

You can save a program by selecting the **F**ile, **S**ave option which will save your program automatically with the same name as that used when loaded, or if the name of the program is 'Untitled', you will be asked to provide a name to save it under. The filename you type in must not be longer that 8 alphanumeric characters (letters and numbers). QuickBASIC will add automatically the .BAS three letter extension.

If you wish to save a program under a different name than the one given to it from an earlier **S**ave, then use the **F**ile command, followed by the Save **A**s... option which displays a dialogue box, asking you for the name of the file to be saved as. Do remember to give the drive/path specification, if different from the default.

Problem 1.1

Write a program, using the INPUT statement, which can convert degrees Fahrenheit (F) to degrees Celsius (C). Use the following relationship:

Degrees Celsius=(Degrees Fahrenheit−32)*5/9

Exercises

1. The following assignment statements contain at least one error. Identify them.

```
ALPHA = 5.X+BETA
SQUARE = 1.55/-2.44*G^2
VALUE-3.96 = X^1.6
3.14 = PI
DENOMINATOR = X**N/M
X = (A+6)*^2
-ZETA = A+B
NUMBER = K/^X
ROW = 16.5K+1
COLUMN = 2*-X+1
```

2. In each of the following expressions, the variables used have the following values:

Variable	A	B	C	D	E	F	G
Value	5	3	8	4	7	2	6

Use your computer in immediate mode to work out the correct answer to the expressions given below. To arrive at the final answer, calculate all intermediate steps in the order dictated by the priority procedure.

```
X1=A*B^E+F
X2=A*B^(E+F)
X3=A*B/C*D
X4=A*B/(C*D)
X5=A+B*G+C*G^2+D*G^3
X6=(A+B)*G+C*G^2+D*G^3
X7=(A^F+(B-1/C)^F)^0.5
X8=(A^F+B-1/C^F)^0.5
X9=A/B^2-C*D/((E+F)+G^3)
```

To check your answers, write a program which assigns values to A, B, C, etc., and then solves the expressions.

3. Write a program, using the INPUT statement, which can convert gallons into litres. Use the relationship

1 gallon = 4.54609 litres.

2. INPUT & OUTPUT CONTROL

A program can be made to assign values to variables by either entering information on the keyboard, reading information from data statements, or reading information from data files. Output can be directed to the display screen, sent to the printer or written into a file. Reading input from a data file and writing output to a data file will be dealt with in a separate section.

The INPUT Statement:
The INPUT statement is used to enter data from the keyboard. We have already used this statement earlier on, but we will examine it more thoroughly here. This will be illustrated by writing a program to calculate 15% of any number. The number itself is entered via the INPUT statement, as shown below.

```
REM PERCENT PROGRAM
INPUT Number
Rate=15
Value=Number*Rate/100
PRINT Value
END
```

The INPUT statement, as written above, causes BASIC to halt execution, print a question mark (?) and wait for the user to type in a numerical value. Use the editor to enter this program into your computer and then press the **F5** function key to run it. When the computer prints the question mark, type 300 (and don't forget to press the <Enter> key). BASIC will execute the remaining statements in the program and will print

```
45
```

on the screen.

The program can be made more general by using a second INPUT statement to assign a value to the variable Rate. In this way, any percentage of any number can be calculated. To avoid making mistakes in our responses we can include a prompt (message) in the INPUT statement. For example, change the second and third lines of the program to the following:

```
INPUT "Enter a Number ",Number
INPUT "Enter % ",Rate
```

On **Run**ning the program, BASIC will write

```
Enter a Number _
```

with the cursor positioned as shown. If we type 400 (say), the next line will be executed, and BASIC will write

```
Enter % _
```

and wait for a number. Typing 10 (say), causes the rest of the program lines to be executed and BASIC displays

```
40
```

Note: When a delimited prompt (called a string) is included in an INPUT statement, the question mark printed by QuickBASIC is suppressed if a comma is used to separate the string from the list of variables. If this comma is substituted by a semicolon, then QuickBASIC prints the question mark.

Save this program for future use, under the file name PERCENT.

The READ & DATA Statements:

In previous examples, values were assigned to variables either within the program or through the use of the INPUT statement; if more variables were needed, more such assignments were made. In programs requiring many variables and constants, especially when they are not expected to change between each run, the READ and DATA statements should be used.

The DATA statement introduces a numeric constant, or a series of constants, into a program. The READ statement links variable names sequentially with the constant values supplied by the DATA statement. READ and DATA statements must accompany one another within a program, but they need not be paired. If five variables appear in one or more READ statements, there must be at least five constants in one or more DATA statements.

If the total number of constants in all DATA statements is less than the total number of variables in all READ statements, BASIC will respond with an error message which indicates lack of data. Excess data are ignored.

In the following example, all data is introduced in a single DATA statement. It is used at separate points in the program by two READ statements.

```
REM USE OF READ STATEMENT
READ A,B
X=A+B
PRINT A,B,X
READ C,D
Y=C+D
PRINT C,D,Y
DATA 1,5,2,6
END
```

On **Run**ning this program, BASIC will respond by writing

```
1   5   6
2   6   8
```

In executing such a program, BASIC ignores all DATA statements (even if such statements appear on lines preceding the READ statements) until it encounters a READ statement. It then goes back to the first line of the program and starts to search for a DATA statement. Here it finds one in the penultimate line of the program. Taking constant values sequentially, it associates them with variables in the READ statement, also taken sequentially: A is assigned a value of 1, and B a value of 5. After leaving a pointer at the next data element, 2, it reverts to the next executable statement following the READ. On reaching the second READ statement, BASIC does not search for the DATA statement, but refers to its pointer to obtain the next unused data element, which is 2. Variables C and D are therefore assigned the values 2 and 6.

The RESTORE Statement:
The RESTORE statement has no parameters or options. It simply makes it possible to recycle through DATA statements beginning with the first DATA line in the program. The following example illustrates its use.

```
REM USE OF RESTORE
READ A,B
PRINT A,B
RESTORE
READ C,D
PRINT C,D
DATA 2,7
END
```

On **Run**ning the program BASIC will write

```
2    7
2    7
```

The RESTORE statement allows the second READ statement to obtain values from the DATA statement, even though the same values were used previously by the first encountered READ statement. Without the RESTORE statement, an error message indicating lack of data for the second READ statement would have occurred. The statement merely moves the data list pointer back to the beginning of the data list. It is ignored in programs which do not contain READ and DATA statements.

Problem 2.1

Write a program, using the READ and DATA statements, which assigns three numbers to the variables Days, Hours and Minutes and then calculates and prints the total number of minutes involved.

The PRINT Statement

In all previous examples variables within a PRINT statement were separated by commas. This caused the values of these variables to be displayed on the same line, left-justified within inbuilt print zones. Integer numbers are displayed in five print zones, the first four having a width of 14 characters, while the last has a width of 24 characters, making altogether 80 characters across the screen. However, long integers or floating-point numbers which are longer than 14 characters will occupy more than one printing zone, which diminishes the number of values that can be printed on one line.

If variables within a PRINT statement are separated by semicolons, BASIC writes their value close together with two intervening spaces.

If a string is included within a PRINT statement, on execution BASIC displays the actual characters within the quotation marks exactly as they appear in the statement. It is a way of providing captions or headings for the computer's output. For example, a better version of the PERCENT program is given on the next page (**S**ave it as PERCENT1).

```
REM GENERAL PERCENT1
INPUT "Enter Number ", Number
INPUT "Enter % ", Rate
Value=Number*Rate/100
PRINT Rate;"% of"; Number; "="; Value
END
```

On **Run**ning the above program and entering the same numeric values for Number and Rate as previously, the computer will write

```
10 % of 400 = 40
```

providing a more meaningful output.

Note that if we were to replace the comma following the prompt string within the INPUT statement in a program by a semicolon or a space, BASIC would display a question mark at the end of the prompt when the statement is executed.

Formatted Output:

Presentation of results can be made very much easier to understand by using the PRINT TAB statement which allows output to be displayed in columns. There are 80 tabulation positions on each of the 25 lines available on your screen. The program below illustrates the use of this statement.

```
REM USE OF PRINT TAB
READ A,B,C,D
PRINT TAB(5); "A"; TAB(10); "B"; TAB(15); "C"; TAB(20); "D"
PRINT TAB(4); A; TAB(9); B; TAB(14); C; TAB(19); D
DATA 15, 25, 10, 20
END
```

On **Run**ning this program BASIC will respond by writing

```
A       B       C       D
15      25      10      20
```

When using TAB with numbers, don't forget to take into account the space required for its sign (– or +). Positive numbers are preceeded with a space rather than the plus sign.

Another formatting function is the PRINT SPC statement which provides a number of spaces between the last printed position and the next one. For example, the first PRINT line of the previous program can be replaced by

```
PRINT SPC(4); "A"; SPC(4); "B"; SPC(4); "C"; SPC(4); "D"
```

The PRINT TAB or PRINT SPC statements cannot be used to move to the left of a current printing position in a given line. Only progressive moves to the right are obeyed.

Note: Although tabulation using the TAB and SPC statements can work very well with whole numbers, using this method to format tables with floating-point numbers doesn't always work because of the number of significant digits.

Problem 2.2

Modify the AVERAGE program, discussed in the previous chapter, by incorporating the PRINT TAB statement so that the output appears in tabular form, under appropriate headings as shown below:

```
VALUES:     A     B     C     AVERAGE
```

QuickBASIC supports one additional tabulation statement, which is:

```
LOCATE Y,X
```

where Y is the vertical position on the screen (1-25) and X is the horizontal position on the screen (1-80). This positions the cursor at any point on the screen, and printing starts on that location, irrespective of the cursor's previous position. To illustrate its use, clear the screen with the CLS (CLear Screen) command. The CLS command clears the screen and sends the cursor to the upper left-hand corner of the screen.

The CLS command is incorporated in the program given below which prints the letter X in the middle of the screen. To see it, select **Alt+R**, followed by <Enter>.

```
REM USE OF CLS
REM AND LOCATE Y,X
CLS
LOCATE 12,40
PRINT "X"
END
```

The LOCATE Y,X statement in the following program places an asterisk at each corner of the monitor's screen. Allowance is made for the appearance of the cursor at the bottom of the screen, after the execution of the program, which has the effect of scrolling the information on the screen upwards by a line.

Note that in order to counteract line scrolling of information on the screen, we LOCATE the cursor to position 2 in the Y-direction, instead of position 1 when placing the asterisks at the top corners of the screen, and to position 79 in the X-direction, instead of position 80 when placing the asterisks at the right edge of the screen.

```
REM PLACING ASTERISKS AT CORNERS OF SCREEN
CLS
LOCATE 2,1
PRINT "*";
LOCATE 2,79
PRINT "*"
LOCATE 24,1
PRINT "*";
LOCATE 24,79
PRINT "*"
END
```

The PRINT USING Statement

The PRINT USING statement can be used to display numeric information in a variety of formats. A typical format would be:

```
PRINT USING "#####,###.##"; Variable_name
```

which would reserve a field of 12 characters (indicated by the 10 hashes, the comma and the period) in which to display the value of Variable_name, right justified within that field, rounded to two decimal places, with commas preceding groups of three digits to the left of the decimal point. For example, if Variable_name held the numeric value 12345.67 and the above statement was used to print it, BASIC would display the number in the form 12,345.67.

The backslash character can be used to format text. For example,

```
PRINT USING "\□□□□□□\"; Text$
```

will display the first 8 characters (six spaces indicated above by small boxes so that you can see them and two backslashes) of the string held in Text$.

If the exclamation mark (!) is used between the quotes, then the first character of the string Text$ is displayed at the position where the exclamation mark was placed.

A mixture of text and numeric information can be used in a format statement as shown in the program below. But before you type in the program below, first **Run** the program which is the solution to Problem 2.2, but this time supply it with the following floating-point numbers:

```
22.35, 15.32, 14.14
```

On pressing <Enter>, the display will look as follows:

```
Enter three numbers 22.35, 15.32, 14.14
VALUES:       A          B          C          AVERAGE
              22.35
                         15.32
                                    14.14
                                               17.27
```

the layout of which can hardly be called satisfactory! Now enter the program below (which is an adaptation of the program we have been discussing above) into your computer.

```
REM FORMATTED AVERAGES
INPUT "Enter three numbers ", A, B, C
Sum=A+B+C
Average=Sum/3
PRINT "VARIABLES:   A     B     C     AVERAGE"
Form$="\          \###.## ###.## ###.##    ###.##"
PRINT USING Form$; "VALUES ARE:", A; B; C; Average
END
```

On executing this program and supplying it with the same values for variables A, B and C, the following display is obtained:

```
Enter three numbers 22.35, 15.32, 14.14
VARIABLES:        A         B          C              AVERAGE
VALUES ARE:   22.35     15.32      14.14                17.27
```

with the numbers right-justified within their given fields of six characters. The relative spacing of the variable names in the first PRINT statement with respect to the statement following it, is very important. Do try it.

Additional formatting strings which can be used within the PRINT USING statement are incorporated as examples in the program below. However, before you start entering the program into your computer, read the next paragraph first.

Note: In program listings presented in this book from this point on, it is sometimes necessary to break a long BASIC line into two, or more, text lines because of the width limitations imposed by the book layout. The continuation line(s) of such code is indented by at least six spaces so that it is easily recognisable. However, when typing such program lines into the editor, make sure they are entered as <u>one line</u> only, otherwise an error will be generated.

```
REM FORMATTING WITH PRINT USING
P$="Value held in Number"
Number=256.518
PRINT USING "! is the first letter in the prompt string"; P$
PRINT USING "\   \ is the first word in the prompt string"; P$
PRINT USING "& is the whole of the prompt string"; P$
PRINT USING "Value ####.### is in floating point form"; Number
PRINT USING "Value +####.### is in signed floating point form";
            Number
```

```
PRINT USING "Value #.####^^^^ is in exponential form";
        Number
PRINT USING "Value £###.## is in currency form"; Number
PRINT USING "Value #### is in integer form"; Number
END
```

On running the above program, the following output

```
V is the first letter in the prompt string
Value is the first word in the prompt string
Value held in Number is the whole of the prompt string
Value  256.518 is in floating point form
Value  +256.518 is in signed floating point form
Value 0.2565E+03 is in exponential form
Value £256.52 is in currency form
Value  257 is in integer form
```

is displayed on the screen.

Outputting to Printer

Changing all PRINT commands to LPRINT causes all output to be sent to the printer rather than the screen.

Associated with the LPRINT statement is the WIDTH command which is used to specify the maximum number of characters to be printed on each line before performing a carriage return and line feed. The statement is of the form

```
WIDTH "LPT1:",n
```

where n is the number of characters to be printed on each line, the default value being 80.

Exercises

1. Write a program to read a number and then calculate and print under suitable headings, the original number and the discounted values at 12.5%, 15% and 17.5% of the original value.

2. Write a program to calculate the cost of electricity at 5.5 pence per unit between quarterly meter readings Low_value and Hi_value which represent the 'low meter reading value' and the 'high meter reading value'. The flat quarterly charge, irrespective of units used, is £8.85.

   Use the INPUT statement to assign values to variables Low_value and Hi_value, and the READ statement to assign values to variables Unit_cost and Flat_rate.

3. Write a program which calculates the area of a circle, the surface area of a sphere and the volume of a sphere, given the radius R.

   The output should appear on one line under appropriate captions.

4. Write a program to read in a positive floating-point number into a variable called Value, place the integral part of it into variable Integ, and the fractional part of it into variable Fract. Print out the original number, and the integral and fractional parts of it under appropriate headings.

5. The values of six variables are to be printed on one line. Variables A and B are floating-point and are to be printed in a field of 12 each with two digits after the decimal point, variables K and L are integers and are to be printed in a field of 10 each, and variables X and Y are exponential and are to be printed in a field of 16 each with six digits after the decimal point. Write appropriate statements to achieve the layout of this print.

6. Modify the program of Problem 2.1, by using appropriate formatting controls so that the output appears in tabular form, under appropriate headings as shown below:

   DAYS   HOURS   MINUTES   TOTAL_MINUTES

3. CONTROL OF PROGRAM FLOW

QuickBASIC can force a section of code to be repeated by the use of the FOR...NEXT loop, in the same way as other standard BASICs, or by the use of the WHILE...WEND loop, in the same way as other enhanced versions of Basic. In addition to these, QuickBASIC upgrades the WHILE...WEND loop with the use of the DO loop, which tests for a condition either at the beginning or the end of the loop.

In standard BASIC decisions are made with the use of the IF...THEN statement, while in advanced versions of it the IF...THEN...ELSE, ON...GOTO, and ON...GOSUB statements are also used. QuickBASIC advances these by the addition of the block IF...ELSE...ENDIF and SELECT CASE statements.

The FOR...NEXT Loop

The FOR and NEXT statements are used to mark the beginning and ending points of program loops. Any statements between the FOR and its corresponding NEXT will be executed repeatedly according to the conditions supplied by the 'control variable' within the FOR statement. An example is given below.

```
REM USE OF FOR...NEXT LOOP
FOR K=1 TO 5 STEP 1
    PRINT K
NEXT K
END
```

Within the FOR statement, the control variable K is assigned the value 1 which is increased repeatedly by the number following STEP until it reaches 5. It thus has the values 1, 2, 3, 4 and 5. Since it cannot have these values simultaneously, a loop is formed beginning with the FOR and ending with the NEXT. The statements within the loop are executed five times, each time with a new value for K. The NEXT statement increases the value of K and causes repeated jumps to the FOR statement until K exceeds its final assigned value of 5. When this happens, control passes to whatever statement follows the NEXT statement (in this case END).

Note that the PRINT statement, which occurs between the FOR and NEXT statements, is indented. Indentation simply improved readability of the program and has no effect on the compiler - it is simply a good programming style and will, therefore, be adopted in all future program listings.

The following program makes use of the FOR...NEXT loop, as well as an accumulator, to find the sum of a list of numbers.

```
REM SUM OF N NUMBERS
READ N
Sum=0
FOR I=1 TO N STEP 1
     READ Value
     Sum=Sum+Value
NEXT I
PRINT "Sum of"; N; "numbers =";
PRINT USING "####.##"; Sum
DATA 5, 20.5, 21.3, 20.8, 20.6, 21.1
END
```

On **Run**ning this program, N is assigned the value 5 which is the total number of entries requiring summation. The accumulator Sum is then zeroed, and a FOR...NEXT loop is set up. Note that the limits of the control variable in the FOR statement can be written in terms of other variables. In this case, the highest value is represented by N (the total number of data). Within the loop, each number is read into Value and accumulated into Sum. Once the loop is completed, variable Sum holds the summation of all the numbers. The PRINT statements cause Basic to write

```
Sum of 5 numbers = 104.30
```

on the screen.

Use of STEP:

In the last example, the STEP modifier was equal to +1. When this is the case, the STEP modifier can be omitted and the FOR statement can be written as

```
FOR I=1 TO N
```

in which case it is assumed that the STEP is equal to +1.

If the step value desired is not equal to +1, the STEP modifier must be included. For example,

```
REM CONVERT INCHES TO CENTIMETRES
PRINT "INCHES", "CENTIMETRES"
FOR Inches=5 TO 20 STEP 5
    Centimetres=2.54*Inches
    PRINT USING "###.##"; Inches; TAB(17); Centimetres
NEXT Inches
END
```

will convert 5, 10, 15 and 20 inches into centimetres. The output should be as follows:

```
INCHES    CENTIMETRES
  5.00       12.70
 10.00       25.40
 15.00       38.10
 20.00       50.80
```

A negative STEP modifier is legal in Basic. For example,

```
FOR J=5 TO 1 STEP -1
    PRINT J
NEXT J
END
```

will print the values 5, 4, 3, 2 and 1.

For positive step values, the loop is executed so long as the control variable is less than or equal to its final value. For negative step values the loop continues as long as the control variable is greater than or equal to its final value. The statements within the FOR...NEXT loop in the following program will not be executed at all, as the final value of the step modifier is less than the initial value and a positive STEP is indicated.

```
FOR I=1 TO 0 STEP 1
    PRINT "Loop done "; I; " times"
NEXT I
PRINT "Finished"
END
```

Infinite Looping:
A condition of infinite looping can be created by specifying 0 (zero) for the step modifier. However, before you experiment with this, make sure that you have set BREAK ON in your **config.sys** file, otherwise you will not be able to stop program execution with **Ctrl+Break**. Having done this, then change the FOR statement of the above program to

```
FOR I=1 TO 5 STEP 0
```

On execution column 1 of the screen fills up with 'Loop done 1 times' and the program will happily go on for ever until you press **Ctrl+Break**.

Nested FOR...NEXT Loops:
FOR...NEXT statements can be nested to allow the programming of loops within loops as shown in the example below:

```
REM NESTED FOR-NEXT LOOPS
FOR K=1 TO 9
    FOR L=K TO 9
     PRINT USING "#"; L;
    NEXT L
    PRINT
NEXT K
END
```

On **Run**ning this program, two loops are set up as follows:

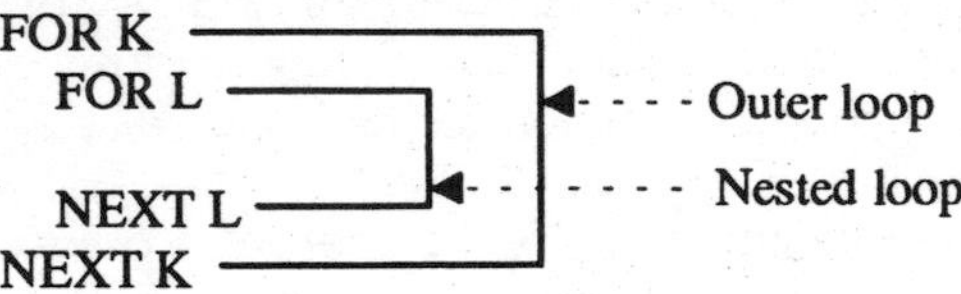

The outer loop is initialized with K=1 and, immediately, the inner, nested loop is executed 9 times. Then the control variable K is incremented by 1, so that now K=2 and the nested loop is executed 8 times. This is repeated until K is equal to 9, when the nested loop is executed only once.

The output of this program is as follows:

```
123456789
23456789
3456789
456789
56789
6789
789
89
9
```

The semicolon after the variable L in the PRINT USING statement allows output to be printed close together on the same line. However, each line of print must be terminated with a line feed (that is, it must send the computer display to the next line). This is provided here by the empty PRINT statement. Without it all the numbers now appearing on different lines would be printed on the same line.

Problem 3.1

Modify the above program so that the output is a square of 15x15 characters positioned in the middle of the screen, and using the letter X as the output character.

Additional levels of nesting are possible. However, deep nesting is costly in terms of memory space. Fig. 3.1 shows some loop configurations, the first five of which are examples of allowable loops, while the sixth is not. Lines joining FOR...NEXT statements must not cross.

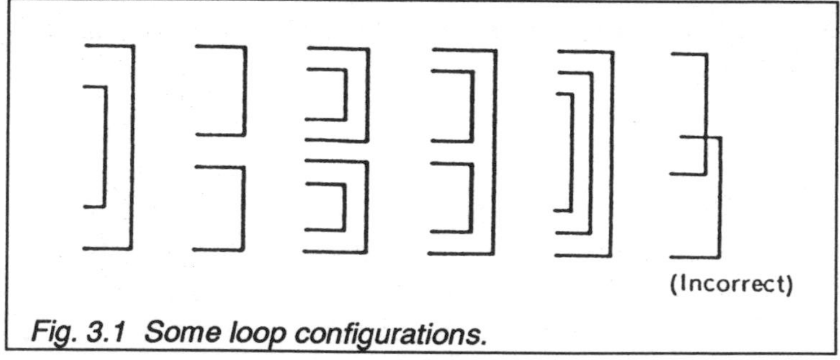

Fig. 3.1 Some loop configurations.

It is bad programming practice to exit a FOR...NEXT loop which has not been completed. Programs may work when you do this but the results are unpredictable. However, if such an exit is unavoidable, then make sure you use the EXIT FOR command (more about this later).

The DO Loop

The DO loop provides a method of looping through a block of statements and has several variations; it can either check the condition after or before executing the block of statements.

The DO...LOOP UNTIL Configuration:

In this configuration the DO marks the beginning of the loop, while the LOOP UNTIL marks the end. Any statements between the DO and its corresponding LOOP UNTIL will be executed repeatedly until the trailer of the LOOP UNTIL statement is true.

To illustrate the use of this loop configuration, load the PERCENT1 program and edit it so that it is the same as the one shown below:

```
REM GENERAL PERCENT2
INPUT "Enter number (-1 to END) ", Number
DO
    INPUT "Enter % ", Rate
    Value=Number*Rate/100
    Form$="###.# %OF #,###.## = ###.##"
    PRINT USING Form$; Rate, Number, Value
    PRINT
    INPUT "Enter number (-1 to END) ", Number
LOOP UNTIL Number<0
END
```

All statements between the DO and LOOP UNTIL lines are repeated UNTIL the trailer of UNTIL is true (that is, until you type a negative value in response to the prompt "Enter number").

Note that, in this case, the condition is checked after the statements in the block have been executed at least once. Therefore typing -1 the first time round will not end the program.

The DO UNTIL...LOOP Configuration:
In this configuration the loop repeats the block of statements as long as a certain condition is true. For example, the above program can be rewritten as:

```
REM GENERAL PERCENT3
INPUT "Enter number (-1 to END) ", Number
DO UNTIL Number<0
     INPUT "Enter % ", Rate
     Value=Number*Rate/100
     Form$="###.# %OF #,###.## = ###.##"
     PRINT USING Form$; Rate, Number, Value
     PRINT
     INPUT "Enter number (-1 to END) ", Number
LOOP
END
```

Here, typing –1 the first time round, ends the program.

The DO...LOOP WHILE Configuration:
In this loop configuration, the WHILE statement can be used in place of the UNTIL statement, provided the relational test has been replaced by its opposite. For example the PERCENT2 program will have to be changed to what is shown below, to produce the same logical behaviour as the program from which it was derived.

Note that the relational test has been changed from less than zero (<0) to greater or equal to zero (>=0). These and other relational operators will be discussed shortly.

```
REM GENERAL PERCENT4
INPUT "Enter number (-1 to END) ", Number
DO
     INPUT "Enter % ", Rate
     Value=Number*Rate/100
     Form$="###.# %OF #,###.## = ###.##"
     PRINT USING Form$; Rate, Number, Value
     PRINT
     INPUT "Enter number (-1 to END) ", Number
LOOP WHILE Number>=0
END
```

The DO WHILE...LOOP Configuration:
Similarly, the PERCENT3 program will have to be changed to

```
REM GENERAL PERCENT5
INPUT "Enter number (-1 to END) ", Number
DO WHILE Number>=0
    INPUT "Enter % ", Rate
    Value=Number*Rate/100
    Form$="###.# % OF #,###.## = ###.##"
    PRINT USING Form$; Rate, Number, Value
    PRINT
    INPUT "Enter number (-1 to END) ", Number
LOOP
END
```

to produce the same logical behaviour as the program from which it was derived.

Problem 3.2

Compound interest can be calculated using the formula

$$A = P * (1+R/100)^n$$

where P is the original money lent, A is what it amounts to in n years at R per cent per annum interest.

Write a program to calculate the amount of money owed after n years, where n changes from 1 to 15 in yearly increments, if the money lent originally is £5,000 and the interest rate remains constant throughout this period at 11.5%. Format the output so as to restrict calculated values to two decimal places and tabulate the results.

The WHILE...WEND Loop

The WHILE...WEND loop is another possible configuration, mostly available in enhanced versions of Basic. It is of the general form:

```
WHILE <relational test is true>
    { execute this }
    {  block of  }
    { statements }
WEND
```

This loop configuration produces the same logical behaviour as that of the DO WHILE...LOOP. In order to illustrate the point, the PERCENT5 program is rewritten below with appropriate changes included.

Use the editor and make the suggested changes to these programs and verify for yourself that they work as they should.

```
REM GENERAL PERCENT6
INPUT "Enter number (-1 to END) ", Number
WHILE Number>=0
     INPUT "Enter % ", Rate
     Value=Number*Rate/100
     Form$="###.# % OF #,###.## = ###.##"
     PRINT USING Form$; Rate, Number, Value
     PRINT
     INPUT "Enter number (-1 to END) ", Number
WEND
END
```

The IF Statement

The IF statement allows conditional program branching. To illustrate the point, edit the PERCENT2 program to:

```
REM GENERAL PERCENT7
DO
     INPUT "Enter number (-1 to END) ", Number
     IF Number<0 THEN END
     INPUT "ENTER % ", Rate
     Value=Number*Rate/100
     Form$="###.# % OF #,###.## = ###.##"
     PRINT USING Form$; Rate, Number, Value
     PRINT
LOOP UNTIL Number <0
```

On **Run**ning the program, you could now stop execution by simply entering -1 in response to the "Enter number" prompt. When this IF statement is encountered, the value of variable Number is compared with the constant appearing after the relational operator (<). If the test condition is met, the trailer of the IF statement is executed (in this case END). If, however, the test condition is not met, the next statement after the IF statement is executed (in this case the INPUT statement).

Note: The inclusion of the IF...THEN statement in the form adopted above, has made the trailer of the LOOP UNTIL statement (Number <0) redundant; it merely acts as a device to force looping. In such cases we could use any variable as trailer. We could, for example, use

```
LOOP UNTIL False
```

False is a built-in BASIC variable and its value is zero. This will cause repeated looping, since the variable used as trailer is set to zero. If it had any other value, looping would halt.

The IF...THEN...END IF Statement:
The form of the IF...THEN statement used previously only supports one statement as the trailer to it. However, it could be that under certain conditions we need to execute more than one statement as a result of conditional program branching. In such a case we could use the QuickBASIC's advanced form of the block IF...THEN statement, which has the following general form:

```
IF <relational test is true> THEN
    { execute these }
    {  statements   }
END IF
```

To illustrate the point, refer to the program below.

```
REM AVERAGE OF N NUMBERS
INPUT "Enter number of values to be averaged ", Total
IF Total>0 THEN
    Sum=0
    FOR K=1 TO Total
     PRINT "Value No. "; K;
     INPUT Value
     Sum=Sum+Value
    NEXT K
    Average=Sum/Total
    Form$="Average of ### numbers = ###.##"
    PRINT USING Form$; Total, Average
END IF
PRINT "Finished"
END
```

The previous program calculates the average of a predefined number of values. First it asks you to enter the Total number of values you require to average, before asking for the individual values. When QuickBASIC encounters this IF statement, it compares the value of the variable Total with the constant appearing after the relational operator (in this case the > sign). If the test condition is met, the trailer of the IF statement is executed (in this case all the statements between the IF and END IF statements. If, however, the test condition is not met, the statement following the END IF statement is executed (in this case the PRINT statement prior to the END).

The IF statement here acts as a guard against an attempt to enter a zero for Total which would result in a zero being divided by zero when working out the average. **S**ave this program under the filename IFENDIF.

Relational Operators within IF Statements:
The table below shows all the relational operators allowed within an IF statement.

Relational Operators

BASIC symbol	*Example*	*Meaning*
=	A = B	A equal to B
<	A < B	A less than B
<=	A <= B	A less than or equal to B
>	A > B	A greater than B
>=	A >= B	A greater than or equal to B
<>	A <> B	A not equal to B

The power of the IF statement is increased considerably by the combination of several relational expressions with the logical operators

```
AND OR XOR NOT EQV and IMP
```

We can write the statement

```
IF X>3 AND M=5 THEN
```

which states that only if both relational tests are met will the trailer of the IF statement be executed.

Another example is

```
IF X>3 OR M=5 THEN
```

which states that when either or both relational test(s) are true, then the trailer of the IF statement will be executed, while the statement

```
IF X>3 XOR M=5 THEN
```

states that when either relational test is true, but not both, then the trailer of the IF statement will be executed. Finally, the statement

```
IF NOT(X<12) THEN
```

has the same effect as IF X>=12 THEN in which the relational test is the negation of that in the above.

The IF...THEN...ELSE Statement:
In many cases we have to perform an IF statement twice over to detect which of two similar conditions is true. This is illustrated below.

```
REM THE TWO IF STATEMENTS
INPUT "Enter a number within 1 to 99 ", N
IF N < 10 THEN
     PRINT "One digit number"
END IF
IF (N > 9) THEN
     PRINT "Two digit number"
END IF
END
```

A more advanced version of the IF statement allows both actions to be inserted in its trailer. An example of this is incorporated in the modified program below:

```
REM USE OF THE IF..THEN..ELSE STATEMENTS
INPUT "Enter a number within 1 to 99 ", N
IF (N < 10) THEN
     PRINT "One digit number"
ELSE
     PRINT "Two digit number"
END IF
END
```

Save this program under the filename THENELSE and execute it supplying numbers between 1 and 99. Obviously, if you type in numbers greater than 99 the program will not function correctly in its present form. But assuming that you have obeyed the message and typed 50 the second PRINT statement in the trailer of the IF statement (after the ELSE) will be executed. If the number entered was less than 10, the first PRINT statement after THEN would be executed. The general structure of this block IF is:

```
IF <relational test> THEN
     { execute this }
     {  block of  }
     { statements }
     {  if true   }
ELSE
     { execute this }
     {  block of  }
     { statements }
     {  if false  }
END IF
```

Note: In the above structure, no statements can follow the words THEN and ELSE.

The ELSEIF Statement:
If your programming logic requires the use of the block IF statement to choose amongst several options by, say, using:

```
IF <relational test_1> THEN
     { execute this }
     {    block    }
     {   if true   }
ELSE
     IF <relational test_2> THEN
      { execute this }
      {    block    }
      {   if true   }
     ELSE
      { execute this }
      {    block    }
      {  if false   }
     END IF
END IF
```

then use the ELSEIF statement to simplify the structure of your program to the following:

```
IF <relational test_1> THEN
      {execute this}
      {    block    }
      {   if true   }
      ELSEIF <relational test_2> THEN
       {execute this}
       {    block    }
       {   if true   }
      ELSE
       {execute this}
       {    block    }
       {   if false  }
END IF
```

QuickBASIC's ELSEIF statement makes the whole structure easier to understand.

Simple Data Sorting

The program below allows us to enter two numbers, tests to find out which is the larger of the two and prints them in descending order. It also illustrates some of the points mentioned above.

```
REM TWO NUMBER SORT
DO
      INPUT "Enter two numbers (-1 to END) ", A, B
      IF A = -1 THEN
       PRINT "Finished"
       END
      ELSEIF A >= B THEN
       PRINT A, B
      ELSE
       PRINT B, A
      END IF
LOOP UNTIL False
```

The program can be stopped by entering a negative value for A. Otherwise, A is compared with B and the appropriate PRINT statement is executed.

The sorting problem becomes more complicated, however, if instead of two numbers we introduce a third one. For two number sorting we had two possible PRINT statements (the number of possible permutations being 1*2=2). For three number sorting however, the total number of PRINT statements becomes six (the total possible permutations being equal to 1*2*3=6). The combinations are (A,B,C), (A,C,B), (C,A,B), (C,B,A), (B,C,A) and (B,A,C). Thus, if we were to pursue the suggested logic in dealing with the problem it would result in a very inefficient program.

Here is a way in which, with only two IF statements and one PRINT statement, the same solution to the three-number sorting problem can be achieved. It uses a different logic and it is explained here with the help of three imaginary playing cards (see Fig. 3.2). Assume that you are holding these cards in your hand and you wish to arrange them in descending order. Look at the front two (Fig. 3.2a) and arrange them so that the highest value appears in front. Now look at the back two (Fig. 3.2b) and arrange them so that the highest of these two is now in front. Obviously, if the highest card had been at the back, in the first instance, it would by now have moved to the middle position (as shown in Fig. 3.2c), so a repeat of the whole procedure is necessary to ensure that the highest card is at the front (Fig. 3.2d).

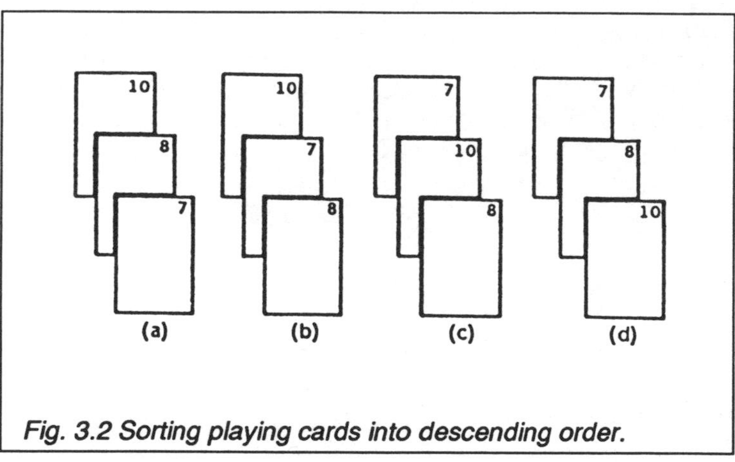

Fig. 3.2 Sorting playing cards into descending order.

The program below achieves this.

```
REM THREE NUMBER SORT
INPUT "Enter three numbers ", A, B, C
WHILE A < B OR B < C
      IF A < B THEN
       Temp=A
       A=B
       B=Temp
      END IF
      IF B < C THEN
       Temp=B
       B=C
       C=Temp
      END IF
WEND
PRINT A, B, C
END
```

The following actions are indicated: If the value in A is less than that in B, exchange them so that the value of A is now stored in B and the value of B is now stored in A. Note, however, that were we to put the value of B into A, we should lose the number stored in A (by overwriting). We therefore transfer the contents of A to a temporary (Temp) variable, then transfer the contents of B to A and finally transfer the contents of Temp to B. The second rotation, necessary when B is less than C, is achieved in a similar manner. The whole process is repeated (with the help of the WHILE...WEND statement), for as long as both A is less than B, or B is less than C. Type this program into the computer under the filename NRSORT.

Problem 3.3

Modify the NRSORT program so that it loops in such a way as to allow repeated execution of the code for different sets of input numbers. Also provide a method of stopping execution.

The SELECT CASE Statement

This is a statement which allows program action to be made dependent on the value of a variable, or an expression. It is QuickBASIC's aid to writing readable programs and provides an efficient alternative to multiple IF statements. The general form of the statement is written as follows:

```
SELECT CASE Expression
     CASE A
      { execute these }
      { statement(s) }
     CASE B TO D
      { execute these }
      { statement(s) }
     CASE E,X
      { execute these }
      { statement(s) }
     CASE ELSE
      { execute these }
      { statement(s) }
END SELECT
```

where Expression can evaluate to either a number or a string. A particular CASE statement within the block (for example, CASE A), will be executed only if Expression evaluates to a constant or a string represented by A.

The following examples will help to illustrate the use of the SELECT CASE structure. The first example evaluates Day (which is the Expression in the general format) to a constant, as follows:

```
REM USING NUMERIC SELECT CASE
INPUT "Enter day number (1-7) ", Day
SELECT CASE Day
     CASE 1 TO 5
      PRINT "Working day"
     CASE 6,7
      PRINT "Weekend"
     CASE ELSE
      PRINT "Not a day"
END SELECT
END
```

The second example evaluates Day$ (which is the Expression in the general format) to a string, as follows:

```
REM USING STRING SELECT CASE
INPUT "Enter first letter of day ", Day$
SELECT CASE Day$
    CASE "M","m","T","t","W","w","F","f"
     PRINT "Working day"
    CASE "S","s"
     PRINT "Weekend"
    CASE ELSE
     PRINT "Not a day"
END SELECT
END
```

Note that both upper and lower case letters must be included in the CASE options in this particular program, if it is to operate correctly under varying input.

Exiting Block Structures

If, for any reason, you require to exit a loop, a function or a procedure prematurely (for example when a data search for a match is successful), then use one of

```
EXIT DO
EXIT FOR
EXIT DEF
EXIT FUNCTION
EXIT SUB
```

the first two being used to exit loops, while the last three to exit functions and procedures.

Problem 3.4

Write a program, using the SELECT CASE structure, that can carry out any of the following conversions:

(a) gallons into litres (1 gallon=4.54609 litres)
(b) feet into metres (1 foot=0.3048 metres)
(c) pounds into kilograms (1 pound=0.453592 kilogram)

Use READ statements to assign the conversion constants to appropriate variables, and the INPUT statement for entering the value to be converted and the type of conversion required.

Exercises

1. Write a program using the FOR...NEXT loop to calculate the squares and cubes of numbers from 1 to 10 inclusive. The results should appear in tabular form under appropriate headings.

2. Modify the compound interest program (see Problem 3.2) so that the annual interest rate is increased by 0.1% after the end of each yearly period.

3. A salesperson receives commission of 10% of their annual sales up to £20,000 and an additional 1% per £1,000 for amounts over £20,000. The maximum commission allowable is however limited to 15%.

   Write a program to calculate the total commission received for annual sales of £19,750, £47,500 and £73,250.

4. Write a program to compute the following expression:

   $$Y = \begin{cases} 1 + (1-x^2) & \text{if } x < 0 \\ 1 - (1+x^2) & \text{if } x > 0 \end{cases}$$

   Use the FOR...NEXT loop to create values for the variable x from –3 to +3 in steps of 0.2.

   Print x and Y for each iteration of the loop, under appropriate headings.

5. Write a program that reads in the examination number of candidates together with their name and the percentage marks attained in a given examination. The marks have to be graded as follows:

   Over 70%, A; 60-69%, B; 50-59%, C; 40-49%, D; Below 40%, F.

   The program should print, under suitable headings, the candidate number, name, mark and grade for each candidate. Arrange for the program to stop when a negative candidate number is entered.

4. STRINGS AND ARRAYS

String Variables

String variables are distinguished from numeric variables by including the **$** tag after their name, or by declaring them as such in a DEFSTR statement. Like numbers, strings can be assigned to variables in several ways. For example, the program below assigns a string to the variable named A$ and then PRINTs A$.

```
A$="ABC123"
PRINT A$
END
```

On **Run**ning the program, Basic writes

```
ABC123
```

on the screen.

The following program will read a string from a DATA statement and assign it to a variable named B$.

```
READ B$
PRINT B$
DATA "A1B2"
END
```

Several strings can be read and assigned to several variables provided that the strings within the DATA statement are separated by commas. In general, string variables can be used within a Basic program in the following statements:

(a) A$="ABC" or A$=B$.
(b) READ A$. The string must be in a DATA statement
(c) INPUT A$
(d) PRINT A$
(e) IF A$="YES" THEN
(f) C$=A$+B$. This is known as 'concatenation'. It simply joins the second string to the end of the first.

Basic assigns a numeric code to each character on the keyboard, according to the ASCII code, as shown in the table below. Thus, each letter of the alphabet is assigned a numeric value and as a result the letter A has a smaller value than B, letter B smaller than C, and so on.

Table of ASCII Conversion Codes

<table>
<tr><th>CHAR</th><th>ABBR</th><th>DEC</th><th>CHAR</th><th>ABBR</th><th>DEC</th><th>CHAR</th><th>ABBR</th><th>DEC</th></tr>
<tr><td>CTRL @</td><td>nul</td><td>0</td><td>CTRL K</td><td>vt</td><td>11</td><td>CTRL V</td><td>syn</td><td>22</td></tr>
<tr><td>CTRL A</td><td>soh</td><td>1</td><td>CTRL L</td><td>ff</td><td>12</td><td>CTRL W</td><td>etb</td><td>23</td></tr>
<tr><td>CTRL B</td><td>stx</td><td>2</td><td>CTRL M</td><td>cr</td><td>13</td><td>CTRL X</td><td>can</td><td>24</td></tr>
<tr><td>CTRL C</td><td>etx</td><td>3</td><td>CTRL N</td><td>so</td><td>14</td><td>CTRL Y</td><td>em</td><td>25</td></tr>
<tr><td>CTRL D</td><td>eot</td><td>4</td><td>CTRL O</td><td>si</td><td>15</td><td>CTRL Z</td><td>sub</td><td>26</td></tr>
<tr><td>CTRL E</td><td>enq</td><td>5</td><td>CTRL P</td><td>dle</td><td>16</td><td>CTRL [</td><td>esc</td><td>27</td></tr>
<tr><td>CTRL F</td><td>ack</td><td>6</td><td>CTRL Q</td><td>dc1</td><td>17</td><td>CTRL \</td><td>fs</td><td>28</td></tr>
<tr><td>CTRL G</td><td>bel</td><td>7</td><td>CTRL R</td><td>dc2</td><td>18</td><td>CTRL]</td><td>gs</td><td>29</td></tr>
<tr><td>CTRL H</td><td>bs</td><td>8</td><td>CTRL S</td><td>dc3</td><td>19</td><td>CTRL ^</td><td>rs</td><td>30</td></tr>
<tr><td>CTRL I</td><td>ht</td><td>9</td><td>CTRL T</td><td>dc4</td><td>20</td><td>CTRL _</td><td>us</td><td>31</td></tr>
<tr><td>CTRL J</td><td>lf</td><td>10</td><td>CTRL U</td><td>nak</td><td>21</td><td></td><td></td><td></td></tr>
<tr><td>SPACE</td><td></td><td>32</td><td>@</td><td></td><td>64</td><td>`</td><td></td><td>96</td></tr>
<tr><td>!</td><td></td><td>33</td><td>A</td><td></td><td>65</td><td>a</td><td></td><td>97</td></tr>
<tr><td>"</td><td></td><td>34</td><td>B</td><td></td><td>66</td><td>b</td><td></td><td>98</td></tr>
<tr><td>#</td><td></td><td>35</td><td>C</td><td></td><td>67</td><td>c</td><td></td><td>99</td></tr>
<tr><td>$</td><td></td><td>36</td><td>D</td><td></td><td>68</td><td>d</td><td></td><td>100</td></tr>
<tr><td>%</td><td></td><td>37</td><td>E</td><td></td><td>69</td><td>e</td><td></td><td>101</td></tr>
<tr><td>&</td><td></td><td>38</td><td>F</td><td></td><td>70</td><td>f</td><td></td><td>102</td></tr>
<tr><td>'</td><td></td><td>39</td><td>G</td><td></td><td>71</td><td>g</td><td></td><td>103</td></tr>
<tr><td>(</td><td></td><td>40</td><td>H</td><td></td><td>72</td><td>h</td><td></td><td>104</td></tr>
<tr><td>)</td><td></td><td>41</td><td>I</td><td></td><td>73</td><td>i</td><td></td><td>105</td></tr>
<tr><td>*</td><td></td><td>42</td><td>J</td><td></td><td>74</td><td>j</td><td></td><td>106</td></tr>
<tr><td>+</td><td></td><td>43</td><td>K</td><td></td><td>75</td><td>k</td><td></td><td>107</td></tr>
<tr><td>,</td><td></td><td>44</td><td>L</td><td></td><td>76</td><td>l</td><td></td><td>108</td></tr>
<tr><td>-</td><td></td><td>45</td><td>M</td><td></td><td>77</td><td>m</td><td></td><td>109</td></tr>
<tr><td>.</td><td></td><td>46</td><td>N</td><td></td><td>78</td><td>n</td><td></td><td>110</td></tr>
<tr><td>/</td><td></td><td>47</td><td>O</td><td></td><td>79</td><td>o</td><td></td><td>111</td></tr>
<tr><td>0</td><td></td><td>48</td><td>P</td><td></td><td>80</td><td>p</td><td></td><td>112</td></tr>
<tr><td>1</td><td></td><td>49</td><td>Q</td><td></td><td>81</td><td>q</td><td></td><td>113</td></tr>
<tr><td>2</td><td></td><td>50</td><td>R</td><td></td><td>82</td><td>r</td><td></td><td>114</td></tr>
<tr><td>3</td><td></td><td>51</td><td>S</td><td></td><td>83</td><td>s</td><td></td><td>115</td></tr>
<tr><td>4</td><td></td><td>52</td><td>T</td><td></td><td>84</td><td>t</td><td></td><td>116</td></tr>
<tr><td>5</td><td></td><td>53</td><td>U</td><td></td><td>85</td><td>u</td><td></td><td>117</td></tr>
<tr><td>6</td><td></td><td>54</td><td>V</td><td></td><td>86</td><td>v</td><td></td><td>118</td></tr>
<tr><td>7</td><td></td><td>55</td><td>W</td><td></td><td>87</td><td>w</td><td></td><td>119</td></tr>
<tr><td>8</td><td></td><td>56</td><td>X</td><td></td><td>88</td><td>x</td><td></td><td>120</td></tr>
<tr><td>9</td><td></td><td>57</td><td>Y</td><td></td><td>89</td><td>y</td><td></td><td>121</td></tr>
<tr><td>:</td><td></td><td>58</td><td>Z</td><td></td><td>90</td><td>z</td><td></td><td>122</td></tr>
<tr><td>;</td><td></td><td>59</td><td>[</td><td></td><td>91</td><td>{</td><td></td><td>123</td></tr>
<tr><td><</td><td></td><td>60</td><td>\</td><td></td><td>92</td><td>|</td><td></td><td>124</td></tr>
<tr><td>=</td><td></td><td>61</td><td>]</td><td></td><td>93</td><td>}</td><td></td><td>125</td></tr>
<tr><td>></td><td></td><td>62</td><td>^</td><td></td><td>94</td><td>~</td><td></td><td>126</td></tr>
<tr><td>?</td><td></td><td>63</td><td>_</td><td></td><td>95</td><td>del</td><td></td><td>127</td></tr>
</table>

Note: In the table above, groups of two or three lower case letters are abbreviations for standard ASCII control characters. Codes within the range 128 to 255 form the extended IBM character set and are not shown.

When strings appear in an IF statement (as in (e) above), they are compared character by character from left to right on the basis of the ASCII values until a difference is found. If a character in that position in string A$ has a higher ASCII code than the character in the same position in string B$, then A$ is greater than B$. If all the characters in the same positions are identical but one string has more characters than the other, the longer string is the greater of the two. Thus, alphabetic strings can be placed easily in alphabetical order.

In the statements given so far, the string variables are considered in their entirety. Later on, however, we shall see that with the help of three special string functions, we can access any character within a given string.

String Arrays

A number of strings can be stored under a common name in what is known as a string array. Let us assume that we have four names e.g. SMITH, JONES, BROWN and WILSON which we would like to store in a string array. In Basic, whenever an array is to be used in a program, you must declare your intention to do so in a DIMension statement as shown in the program below, which allows you to read and store the four names into the common variable Name$().

```
REM USE OF A STRING ARRAY
DIM Name$(4)
FOR I=1 TO 4
    READ Name$(I)
    PRINT Name$(I)
NEXT I
DATA "SMITH" ,"JONES" ,"BROWN" ,"WILSON"
END
```

A simple way to visualize a string array is as follows:

SMITH	JONES	BROWN	WILSON

The four names are stored in a common box which has four compartments (or elements), each compartment containing one name. Thus, Name$(2) refers to the 2nd element of string array Name$(), and Name$(4) to the 4th element.

The DIM statement tells Basic that a string array called Name$() is to be used with maximum dimensions as given within the brackets following the array name (in this case 4). Any reference to an array name within a program must be of the form

```
Name$(I)
```

where I has a value between 0 and the maximum number given in the DIM statement. Note that the statement DIM Name$(4) reserves, in fact, five elements starting with the Name$(0). Reference to Name$ alone does not refer to the array, but to the unsubscripted string variable Name$, which merely happens to be using the same letters.

The following program (written, for the first time, with line numbers so as to make it easier later on to point to required insertions of new statements) will READ from a DATA statement the name, location and telephone extension of five employees. Note that the data have been structured so that the commas separating the names from the locations and the locations from the telephone extensions have the same position within each string. This is achieved by adding spaces to compensate for different lengths of names, etc. We do this at this stage in order to allow manipulation of these strings later.

In this example, the FOR...NEXT loop is written on one line to demonstrate that it is possible to have more than one statement in each program line. If this is the case, statements appearing on one line must be separated by a colon (:). Also note that in this example, two FOR...NEXT loops are used to demonstrate that once data have been READ, they are stored in memory (unless overwritten). One loop would normally be sufficient.

```
10 REM EMPLOYEES
20 DIM Employee$(5)
30 FOR I=1 TO 5: READ Employee$(I): NEXT I
80 FOR I=1 TO 5: PRINT Employee$(I): NEXT I
```

```
310 DATA "WILSON M.  ,ROOM 1.24, 395"
320 DATA "SMITH M.   ,ROOM 2.6  ,7315"
330 DATA "JONES B.M.,ROOM 6.19  ,1698"
340 DATA "SMITH A.A.  ,ROOM 2.12, 456"
350 DATA "BROWN C.   ,ROOM 3.1   , 432"
400 END
```

Type this program using the same line numbers as those given above, **S**ave it under the filename EMPLOY and **R**un it.

Basic will write the literals on the screen as they appear within the DATA statements, but without the quotation marks, as follows:

```
WILSON M. ,ROOM 1.24, 395
SMITH M.   ,ROOM 2.6  ,7315
JONES B.M.,ROOM 6.19,1698
SMITH A.A. ,ROOM 2.12,456
BROWN C. ,ROOM 3.1  , 432
```

String Functions

We shall now introduce some functions which allow string manipulation. For example, suppose we want to extract and print out only the names of the employees held in array Employee$(). Basic allows us to do this quite easily with the function

```
LEFT$()
```

The few program lines given below, when added to the previous program will achieve this.

```
140 PRINT
150 FOR I=1 TO 5
160   PRINT LEFT$(Employee$(I),10)
170 NEXT I
```

Note that the function LEFT$ has two bracketed arguments; first is the Ith string of string array Employee$() and second is the numeral 10 which refers to the number of characters of interest. The function, together with the PRINT statement, causes the 10 leftmost characters of Employee$(I) to be printed. Type these additional lines and try the program.

Another string function allows manipulation of the rightmost characters of a string. This is achieved by the use of the function

```
RIGHT$()
```

To illustrate its use, change line 160 of the program to

```
160 PRINT LEFT$(Employee$(I),10), RIGHT$(Employee$(I),4)
```

and **R**un it. The second column of the last PRINT statement contains the four rightmost characters of each string.

A third function which allows information to be extracted from the middle of a string is

```
MID$()
```

Substituting line 160 in the program with the line given below, will print the location of each employee.

```
160 PRINT MID$(Employee$(I),12,9)
```

Note that this function requires two numeric values to follow the Ith string. The first is the starting point within a string (12th character here) and the second is the number of characters to be considered (9 in this case). If the second number is omitted from the argument list, then the characters considered start at the first number and finish at the end of the string.

As an example of the use of string arrays, consider the program on the next page, which causes information on the quantity and price of several items in stock to be stored by Basic. To extract details on items in stock, simply start the program and answer the questions posed.

Firstly, the program reads and stores into string array Item$() the actual names of the items in stock, while at the same time their quantity and price are read into Stock$(). In response to the question 'WHICH ITEM', the name of an item, associated with the string variable Xname$, is typed in. If it is END, then the program stops. If, however, it has any other name, it causes a FOR...NEXT loop to be set up which compares in turn the contents of Item$() with Xname$. If they are found to be equal, it prints the required information held in Stock$().

```
REM STOCKTAKING
DIM Item$(4), Stock$(4)
FOR I=1 TO 4: READ Item$(I), Stock$(I): NEXT I
DO: PRINT
    INPUT "WHICH ITEM "; Xname$
    IF Xname$="END" THEN END
    FOR I=1 TO 4
     IF Xname$=Item$(I) THEN
       PRINT ">>>>>> "; LEFT$(Stock$(I),3); " IN STOCK
                      AT £"; RIGHT$(Stock$(I),4); " EACH"
     END IF
    NEXT I
LOOP UNTIL False
DATA "INK ERASER", "200,0.10"
DATA "PENCIL ERASER", "320,0.15"
DATA "TYPING ERASER", "25 ,0.25"
DATA "CORRECTION FLUID", "150,0.50"
```

Type this program carefully, paying particular attention to the spaces inserted within the various PRINT and DATA statements, then **S**ave it under filename STOCK. On **Run**ning the program, Basic responds with

```
WHICH ITEM?
```

and awaits your response. Below, we present a typical **R**un.

```
WHICH ITEM? PENCIL

WHICH ITEM? PENCIL ERASER

>>>>>> 320 IN STOCK AT £0.15 EACH

WHICH ITEM? CORRECTION FLUID

>>>>>> 150 IN STOCK AT £0.5 EACH

WHICH ITEM? END
```

which causes the program to end. If you enter information in lower case it will not be recognised in its present form. This can be overcome by changing the two IF statements to

```
IF UCASE$(Xname$)="END" THEN END
IF UCASE$(Xname$)=Item$(I) THEN
```

The function UCASE$() changes the supplied string to 'Upper Case'. The converse to this is LCASE$() which changes the supplied string to 'Lower Case'.

Problem 4.1

Modify the above stocktaking program so that you only need to enter the first three letters of each item in response to the question 'WHICH ITEM'. The output of your program should, however, print the full name of each item. Then, restructure the data so that each data line is read into one element of a string array. Use the LEFT$(), RIGHT$() and MID$() functions to extract appropriate information for the printout.

The need for structuring the data (e.g. with spaces) can lead to mistakes when typing information into a DATA line, especially in the case of numerical data. In fact, numerical data can be stored in a numerical array without the need for structuring them within the DATA statement. This leads to a much greater programming flexibility, and will be investigated in the following section.

Subscripted Numeric Variables

Subscripted variables permit the representation of many quantities with one variable name. A particular quantity is indicated by writing a subscript in parentheses after the variable name. Individual quantities are called elements, while a set of elements is called an array. A subscripted variable may have one, two or three subscripts, and it then represents a one- two- or three-dimensional array.

The elements of a one-dimensional array can be represented as follows:

```
A(0)      A(1)      A(2)      A(3)      A(4)
```

while those of a two-dimensional array as:

```
A(0,0)    A(0,1)    A(0,2)    A(0,3)
A(1,0)    A(1,1)    A(1,2)    A(1,3)
A(2,0)    A(2,1)    A(2,2)    A(2,3)
```

The first of the two subscripts refers to the row number, running from 0 to the maximum number of declared rows, and the second subscript to the column number, running from 0 to the maximum number of declared columns.

A three-dimensional array can be thought of as stacked two-dimensional arrays with the third subscript, running from 0 to the maximum height of the stack.

In the computer, however, arrays are stored with elements following one another on a single line as shown below:

A(0,0) A(1,0) A(2,0) A(0,1) A(1,1) A(2,1)

with the first subscript changing more rapidly than the second, and the second more rapidly than the third (in the case of a three-dimensional array). Provided that this is recognized and understood, we can use the previous pictorial form of representation for programming purposes.

Numerical arrays must be declared prior to their use in a DIM statement just as we had to declare string arrays. The form of the statement is shown below:

```
DIM X(15), Y(3,5), Z(3,5,4)
```

where array X() has been declared to be a one-dimensional array with a maximum of 16 elements (don't forget the zero'th element), array Y(,) has been declared as a two-dimensional array of 4 rows and 6 columns, and array Z(,,) as a three-dimensional array of 4 rows and 6 columns stacked 5 deep. The number of arrays that can be declared simultaneously is dependent only on the available memory in your computer.

QuickBASIC allows range declarations in arrays which greatly enhances their usage. For example, if Array_name1 is the name of a one-dimensional array, and the subscripts are within the range I to J, we must declare this array and its range by using the statement

```
DIM Array_name1(I TO J)
```

Similarly, a two-dimensional array can be declared as

```
DIM Array_name2(K TO L,M TO N)
```

if the elements range from K to L rows and M to N columns.

The following program illustrates the use of numerical arrays. Data are read into a one-dimensional array and subsequently the contents of the even numbered elements are summed into variable Even, while the contents of all the odd elements are summed into variable Odd.

```
REM NUMERICAL ARRAY
DIM Number(15)
REM READ & STORE INTO Number() 16 NUMBERS
FOR I=0 TO 15: READ Number(I): NEXT I
REM SUM EVEN ELEMENTS
Even=0
FOR I=0 TO 14 STEP 2: Even=Even+Number(I): NEXT I
REM SUM ODD ELEMENTS
Odd=0
FOR I=1 TO 15 STEP 2: Odd=Odd+Number(I): NEXT I
REM PRINT CONTENTS OF ARRAY
FOR I=0 TO 15: PRINT Number(I): NEXT I: PRINT
PRINT "EVEN="; Even, "ODD="; Odd
DATA 4, 7, 6, 1, 9, 7, 14, 39, 24, 19, 32, 21, 8, 5, 15, 28
END
```

On **Run**ning this program, the contents of array Number(), which are the numbers listed in the DATA statement, are PRINTed out one under the other. Under these the output

```
EVEN=112  ODD=127
```

appears on the screen.

Static and Dynamic Arrays

QuickBASIC allows you to assign a portion of memory for array use in two different ways. These are:

Static arrays - if the declaration is made with a constant only, for example, DIM Year(1980 TO 2000) or DIM Aname(15)

Dynamic arrays - if (a) the declaration is made with variables, for example, DIM Year(I TO J) or DIM Aname(K);
(b) the word DYNAMIC is inserted in the DIM statement following the word DIM, for example, DIM DYNAMIC Arm(15);

(c) the statement $DYNAMIC appears in the program prior to dimensioning the array.

Static memory is always the same size for each run of the program and cannot be used for any other purpose.

Dynamic memory is allocated during run time and the space may vary for each run of the program. Dynamic memory can be freed at any time for other use with the use of the statement

```
ERASE Array_name
```

However, although dynamic arrays are memory efficient, accessing values held in them is slightly slower that accessing values held in static arrays.

There are two error messages which relate to the use of arrays. These are:

```
Subscript out of range
Overflow
```

The first error occurs if an attempt is made to use an array of more than 10 elements without dimensioning it, or if an attempt has been made to use an array element that is outside the declared dimension, or if an attempt has been made to dimension the array with a negative number of elements. The second error occurs if an attempt is made to use an array for which there is no room in the computer's memory.

We shall now modify the original stocktaking program so that the numerical parts of the data are stored in a two-dimensional array. After you have studied it, carry out the modifications to your version of the stocktaking program resulting from the solution to Problem 4.1.

```
REM STOCKTAKING USING STRINGS AND ARRAYS
DIM Item$(4), Stock(4,2)
FOR I=1 TO 4
    READ Item$(I), Stock(I,1), Stock(I,2)
NEXT I
DO: PRINT
    INPUT "WHICH ITEM "; Xname$
    IF UCASE$(Xname$)="END" THEN END
```

```
        FOR I=1 TO 4
          IF UCASE$(Xname$)=LEFT$(Item$(I),3) THEN
            Form$=">>>>>> \              \### IN STOCK
                    AT £#.## EACH"
            PRINT USING Form$; LEFT$(Item$(I),16), Stock(I,1),
                                    Stock(I,2)
          END IF
        NEXT I
    LOOP UNTIL False
    DATA "INK ERASER", 200, 0.10
    DATA "PENCIL ERASER", 320, 0.15
    DATA "TYPING ERASER", 25 , 0.25
    DATA "CORRECTION FLUID", 150, 0.50
```

Note how much easier it is to structure the DATA statements when using numeric arrays rather than string arrays for numeric data.

Problem 4.2

The first two numbers of the number series given below are 1 and 1. The next number in the sequence is the sum of these two and subsequent numbers are the sum of the preceding pair. So we get:

1, 1, 2, 3, 5, 8, 13, 21, ...

Write a program to calculate the first N numbers of the series (where N is an input to the program) and store them in an appropriate one-dimensional numeric array. In a second one-dimensional array, store the average of adjacent pairs of numbers. Print the output in two columns under appropriate headings.

More String Functions

In this section we shall introduce the following additional string functions:

ASC( ), CHR$( ), LEN( ), STR$( ) and VAL( )

Examples of the use of these functions are given overleaf.

ASCII Conversion:
The use of the ASC() function in the statement

```
N=ASC("ABCD")
```

will return the decimal ASCII code for the first character of the string enclosed in the brackets of the function. In this case, 65 will be returned (see Table on ASCII Conversion Codes).

Character Conversion:
The use of the CHR$() function in the statement

```
C$=CHR$(66)
```

will return the ASCII character that corresponds to the value of the argument, in this case the letter B. The value of the argument must lie between 0 and 255.

Length of String:
The use of the LEN() function in the statement

```
L=LEN("XYZ")
```

will return the value of length of the string, that is, the number of characters in the string. In this case L will be set to 3.

String Conversion:
The use of the STR$() function in the statement

```
S$=STR$(X)
```

will convert the value of the argument into a string. X is a numeric variable which might be the result of a calculation. In this case, if X had the value of 98.56, say, then S$ becomes equal to "98.56".

Value of String:
If R$ represents a string given by

```
R$="3.123E12 METRES"
```

then the statement

```
X=VAL(R$)
```

will return the value of the string up to the first non-numeric character, in this case 3.123E+12. If the string begins with a non-numeric character then the value 0 is returned.

String Concatenation:
Basic allows the concatenation (joining together) of strings. We shall illustrate this facility by considering the following program in which the computer asks you to enter your surname first followed by your first name. It then concatenates the two (first name first followed by surname with a space in between) and prints the result which is held in string variable X$.

```
REM CONCATENATION
CLS:INPUT "Enter your SURNAME please ", S$: PRINT
INPUT "Enter your FIRST NAME please ", N$
X$=N$ + " " + S$
CLS: PRINT "HELLO "; X$
END
```

As it stands, the program is rather trivial. However, using concatenation together with some of the string functions mentioned earlier, can result in a somewhat more spectacular result. To illustrate this, delete the last two lines of the above program and then add the following lines to the program:

```
CLS: L=LEN(X$)
IF L>22 THEN
    X$=LEFT$(N$,1) + ". " + S$
    L=LEN(X$)
END IF
FOR I=1 TO L
    PRINT MID$(X$,I,1);
    IF I=1 THEN PRINT " "; X$;
    IF I=L THEN PRINT " "; X$;
    PRINT TAB(L+4); MID$(X$,I,1)
NEXT I
END
```

Run the program and supply it with your full name (surname first). What you will see on the screen, if your name was JOHN BROWN, is shown on the next page.

```
J JOHN BROWN J
O            O
H            H
N            N

B            B
R            R
O            O
W            W
N JOHN BROWN N
```

Note that the program has worked out the length of your full name and allowed enough space between the two vertical columns to write it horizontally on the first and last rows.

Now **Run** the program again, but this time type in a really long name, say CHRISTOPHER VERYLONGFELLOW. Can you work out from the program lines and the output on your screen what has happened? Try it.

Perhaps the most important use of concatenation is that of building up strings by overlaying. What we mean by this is the ability to create an empty string of a fixed length and then place characters in it anywhere along its length, in any order. The following program will help to illustrate this effect.

```
REM OVERLAYING
A$="*": L$=" "
FOR I=1 TO 40: L$=L$+" ": NEXT I
INPUT "How many stars "; N
FOR I=1 TO N
    DO
     PRINT "Position ";I;: INPUT P
     IF P<1 OR P>40 THEN
      PRINT "RE-Enter"
     ELSE
      EXIT DO
     END IF
    LOOP UNTIL False
    L$=LEFT$(L$,P-1) + A$ + MID$(L$,P+1)
NEXT I: PRINT
PRINT "         1         2         3         4"
PRINT "1234567890123456789012345678901234567890"
PRINT L$
END
```

The first FOR...NEXT loop creates an empty string, L$, 40 characters long. Subsequently, we overlay a number of asterisks (string A$) onto the empty string L$. This is achieved by specifying the position P in which we wish to place an asterisk and concatenating the leftmost P–1 characters already in string L$ to string A$ and then concatenate to the resultant string the remaining characters within string L$ from position P+1 to the end of the string. The result is then stored in L$. The process can be repeated as many times as we choose. Note that unlike the PRINT TAB procedure, with this method we can 'tabulate' backwards.

On **Run**ning the program, Basic will respond with a series of questions. Enter the numbers following the question marks.

```
How many stars ? 3
POSITION 1 ? 35
POSITION 2 ? 24
POSITION 3 ? 12

         1         2         3         4
1234567890123456789012345678901234567890
           *           *          *
```

The numbers above the asterisks are only printed so that we can check the exact position of each asterisk.

Problem 4.3

Write a program which uses one or more string functions to allow:

(a) the printing of a given letter specified by entering a number within the range from 1 to 26, and

(b) the printing of a number corresponding to the position of a given letter within the alphabet, by entering any given letter.

Alphabetical Sorting

Many programming applications, such as manipulation of information on employees' records, require alphabetical sorting. To achieve this, we must draw on the technique developed earlier on for sorting numbers, as well as the 'Three number sort' program.

The technique we shall adopt is more or less the same as the one used previously except that string arrays are used rather than individual variables. This has the effect of reducing the required number of IF statements to one. The technique is illustrated below by applying it to the 'Employees' program which should have been stored under the filename EMPLOY. When changes to the program are made (lines 20-80) and additional program lines are inserted (lines 50-300), your program should look as follows:

```
10 REM ALPHABETICAL SORTING
20 READ N: DIM Employee$(N)
30 FOR I=1 TO N: READ Employee$(I): NEXT I
80 FOR I=1 TO N: PRINT Employee$(I): NEXT I
90 PRINT: PRINT: PRINT "SORTED INFORMATION"
110 FOR I=1 TO N-1
120   IF Employee$(I)>Employee$(I+1) THEN
130     Temp$=Employee$(I+1)
140     Employee$(I+1)=Employee$(I)
150     Employee$(I)=Temp$
160   END IF
170 NEXT I
190 FOR I=1 TO N: PRINT Employee$(I): NEXT I
300 DATA 5
310 DATA "WILSON M.  ,ROOM 1.24 , 395"
320 DATA "SMITH M.   ,ROOM 2.6  ,7315"
330 DATA "JONES B.M.,ROOM 6.19 ,1698"
340 DATA "SMITH A.A.  ,ROOM 2.12 ,456"
350 DATA "BROWN C.  ,ROOM 3.1   ,432"
400 END
```

Make sure that the line numbers of your program correspond to those shown above, as additional lines will shortly be added.

On **Run**ning the above program you will see that the first five lines print the employees in the same order as they appear in the DATA statements. The second five lines are the result of executing the FOR...NEXT loop of statements 110 to 170.

Within this loop, when I=1 the first string is compared with the second and if it is found to be smaller, control is passed to line 160 otherwise the two strings are interchanged (lines 130-150). When I=2 the second string is compared with the third, and so on until I=N−1, when the (N−1)th string is compared with the Nth. The result in our case is that BROWN has moved one position up as follows:

```
WILSON M. ,ROOM 1.24,395
SMITH M.   ,ROOM 2.6  ,7315
JONES B.M.,ROOM 6.19,1698
SMITH A.A. ,ROOM 2.12,456
BROWN C. ,ROOM 3.1  ,432

SORTED INFORMATION
SMITH M.   ,ROOM 2.6  ,7315
JONES B.M.,ROOM 6.19,1698
SMITH A.A. ,ROOM 2.12,456
BROWN C. ,ROOM 3.1  ,432
WILSON M. ,ROOM 1.24,395
```

In order for BROWN to move to the top of the list we must repeat the FOR...NEXT loop of lines 110 to 170, N−1 times. We shall do this by adding an extra FOR...NEXT loop as follows:

```
100 FOR J=1 TO N-1
220 NEXT J
```

Type these two lines into the computer and **Run** the program. You will see that although all the information appears on the screen it is rather difficult to distinguish the result of each execution of the outer FOR...NEXT loop. The addition of the following two lines should put this right.

```
180 PRINT:PRINT J
200 A$=INPUT$(1)
```

The INPUT$(n) statement forces the computer to pause until n characters have been typed on the keyboard before continuing with program execution. This means that the results of each iteration of the J loop can be studied at leisure before continuing with program execution. Add these lines and **Run** the program again.

What you will see on the screen is shown below.

```
SORTED INFORMATION

1
SMITH M.   ,ROOM 2.6  ,7315
JONES B.M.,ROOM 6.19,1698
SMITH A.A. ,ROOM 2.12,456
BROWN C.  ,ROOM 3.1  ,432
WILSON M. ,ROOM 1.24,395

2
JONES B.M.,ROOM 6.19,1698
SMITH A.A. ,ROOM 2.12,456
BROWN C.  ,ROOM 3.1  ,432
SMITH M.   ,ROOM 2.6  ,7315
WILSON M. ,ROOM 1.24,395

3
JONES B.M.,ROOM 6.19,1698
BROWN C.  ,ROOM 3.1  ,432
SMITH A.A. ,ROOM 2.12,456
SMITH M.   ,ROOM 2.6  ,7315
WILSON M. ,ROOM 1.24,395

4
BROWN C.  ,ROOM 3.1  ,432
JONES B.M.,ROOM 6.19,1698
SMITH A.A. ,ROOM 2.12,456
SMITH M.   ,ROOM 2.6  ,7315
WILSON M. ,ROOM 1.24,395
```

The Bubble Sort

From the output of the above program you will notice two things:

(a) After the first execution of the J loop, WILSON drops to the end of the list, and after every subsequent iteration the next highest valued name appears above WILSON.

(b) After each iteration of the J loop, BROWN moves up one position in the list of names.

This means that there is room for improving the program in two ways. Since the highest valued name drops to the bottom of the list, we can reduce the upper limit of the I loop by one for each execution of the J loop. Also, while the full N–1 iterations may be needed in the worst case, the list will often be sorted in somewhere between 0 and N–1 iterations. This can be overcome by incorporating a 'flag' in the program whose value is set to 0 normally, but is reset to 1 every time an exchange takes place. By testing for the value of the flag at the end of each iteration we can tell whether or not we need to execute the J loop once more.

The addition of lines 95, 105, 125 and 205, as well as the change of the variable representing the upper limit of the control variable I in line 110, cover both suggestions for improving the program's efficiency. Finally, as a result of the trailer to the IF statement of line 205, line 400 must be deleted. The resulting program is listed below. Save this program under the filename BUBBLE before executing it.

```
10 REM BUBBLE SORT
20 READ N: DIM Employee$(N)
30 FOR I=1 TO N: READ Employee$(I): NEXT I
80 FOR I=1 TO N: PRINT Employee$(I): NEXT I
90 PRINT:PRINT:PRINT "SORTED INFORMATION"
95 M=N
100 FOR J=1 TO N-1
105 M=M-1: Flag=0
110   FOR I=1 TO M
120     IF Employee$(I)>Employee$(I+1) THEN
125       Flag=1
130       Temp$=Employee$(I+1)
140       Employee$(I+1)=Employee$(I)
150       Employee$(I)=Temp$
160     END IF
170   NEXT I
180   PRINT: PRINT J
190   FOR I=1 TO N: PRINT Employee$(I): NEXT I
200   A$=INPUT$(1)
205   IF Flag=0 THEN END
210 NEXT J
```

```
300 DATA 5
310 DATA "WILSON M. ,ROOM 1.24,395"
320 DATA "SMITH M.   ,ROOM 2.6  ,7315"
330 DATA "JONES B.M.,ROOM 6.19,1698"
340 DATA "SMITH A.A. ,ROOM 2.12,456"
350 DATA "BROWN C.  ,ROOM 3.1   ,432"
```

Variable M is used in line 95 as a temporary store for the total number of strings to be manipulated each time the J loop is executed. Its value is first made equal to N and subsequently it is reduced by one in line 105, thus reducing the value of the upper limit of the control variable I in line 110. This reduces the total number of string comparisons to a minimum.

The constant Flag in lines 105 and 125 is used as an indicator. Its value is set to 1 to indicate that a string interchange has taken place. If Flag remains 0 for the whole of the I loop, then it indicates that the strings are in the required order.

Output to Printer

We have already seen in Chapter 2 that information can be sent to a printer by using the LPRINT statement in place of PRINT. Therefore, to connect the printer from within a Basic program, we must include the LPRINT statement as an option in a decision structure at the appropriate place.

The following program will PRINT the string XYZ on the printer.

```
REM PRINT OUTPUT ON PRINTER
S$="XYZ"
DO
    INPUT "OUTPUT TO SCREEN OR PRINTER? (S/P) ", Q$
LOOP UNTIL UCASE$(Q$)="S" OR UCASE$(Q$)="P"
IF UCASE$(LEFT$(Q$,1))="P" THEN
    LPRINT S$
ELSE
    PRINT S$
END IF
END
```

Problem 4.4

Incorporate the above facility for printing the output of the BUBBLE program either on the screen or on the printer.

Printing to a Device

A glance at the solution to Problem 4.4 will confirm that testing to see whether output should be directed to the screen or the printer and then using PRINT or LPRINT statements can lead to code duplication.

QuickBASIC overcomes such complication by allowing the user to print to a specified device, whether that device is the screen (specified as "SCRN:"), or a line printer (specified as "LPT1:"). This is illustrated by changing appropriately the last program, as follows:

```
REM PRINT TO A DEVICE
S$="XYZ"
DO
    INPUT "OUTPUT TO SCREEN OR PRINTER? (S/P) ", Q$
LOOP UNTIL UCASE$(Q$)="S" OR UCASE$(Q$)="P"
IF UCASE$(LEFT$(Q$,1))="S" THEN
    OPEN "SCRN:" FOR OUTPUT AS #1
ELSE
    OPEN "LPT1:" FOR OUTPUT AS #1
END IF
PRINT #1,S$
END
```

Problem 4.5

Change the solution to Problem 4.4 to incorporate the above facility for printing to a specified device.

Exercises

1. A firm employing 8 persons allows travelling expenses based on the engine capacity of their cars as follows:

   Up to 1199 cc, 15p per mile;
   1200-1499 cc, 19p per mile;
   over 1500 cc, 23p per mile.

   Write a program to read from data statements for each employee, their name, car make, engine capacity of car, and distance travelled each month. The output should appear in tabular form, giving the above information and travelling expenses due.

2. Write a program to calculate the telephone charges for a given list of subscribers and print the results in a tabular form. The table must be sorted in order of subscribers' name and include the name, telephone number, units used and charge.

   The program should read in from DATA statements the names and telephone numbers into a subscripted string array and the units used into a numeric array in the order given in the data lines shown below. The telephone charges are to be calculated at 7 pence per unit.

Names	Phone No.	Units used
Smith A.J.	7141435	300
Jones M.M.	5743129	198
Adams N.P.	8466487	245
Brown J.G.	8673521	843

3. A record is kept of the production of each of the eight machines at a factory. At the end of each week, a data card is prepared for each machine with machine number (from 1 to 8), number of items produced and number of running hours. The information on these cards is then typed into a data file, not necessarily in order of machine number.

Write a program to (a) calculate the number of items produced on each machine per hour, (b) add up the total production, (c) calculate the total hours worked, and (c) calculate the average production per hour. The results should be printed as a list in order of machine number under appropriate headings.

4. A geologist is working with several hundred rock samples which fall into 20 classifications numbered from 1 to 20. Part of the experiment requires recording the weight of each rock sample and producing a table showing the average weight of each classification.

   Assume that data are contained in DATA statements and are structured on N number of lines (N < 1000), each line containing a classification number and a weight in grams, as shown below:

```
DATA 15, 38.5
DATA 11, 155.1
DATA 13, 57.8
DATA 20, 199.3
DATA  1, 45.9
.... .., ...
.... .., ...
```

   Write a program to read the information from the DATA statements, counting the number in each classification and adding up their respective weights, by employing a 20-row by 4-column array with the first column containing the 'classification number', while columns two and three are used for the accumulation of 'numbers in each classification' and 'total weights', as shown below.

   For example, for classification number 15 which occurs only once in the data, the output would be as shown on the next page.

	1	2	3	4
1				
2				
..				
15	15.0	1.0	38.5	
..				
20				

Once the DATA statements have been read and the data processed in the way suggested above, calculate and store the average weight of each classification in the fourth column of the array. Finally, arrange for the information held in the array to be printed out, in matrix form, under suitable headings.

5. FUNCTIONS & PROCEDURES

Standard Arithmetic Functions

QuickBASIC contains functions to perform many mathematical operations. They relieve the user from programming their own small routines to calculate such common functions as logarithms, square roots, sines of angles, and so on. Basic's mathematical functions have a three-letter call name followed by a parenthesised argument. They are predefined and may be used anywhere in a program. Some of Basic's most common standard functions are listed below.

Standard Basic Functions

Call Name	*Function*
ABS(X)	Returns the absolute value of X
ATN(X)	Arc-tangent of X } +1.570796 to −1.570796
COS(X)	Cosine of angle X, where X is in radians
EXP(X)	Raises e to the power of X
INT(X)	Returns the truncated integer part of X
LOG(X)	Returns the natural logarithm of X
SGN(X)	Returns 1, 0 or −1 to reflect the sign of X
SQR(X)	Returns the square root of X
SIN(X)	Sine of angle X, where X is in radians
TAN(X)	Tangent of angle X, where X is in radians
RND	Generates a pseudo-random number from 0 to 1, but which does not include 1.

Function calls can be used as expressions or elements of expressions wherever expressions are legal. The argument X of the function can be a constant, a variable, an expression or another function. A further explanation of the use of these functions is given below.

ATN(X):

The arc-tangent functions return a value in radians, in the range +1.570796 to −1.570796 corresponding to the value of a tangent supplied as the argument X. Conversion to degrees is achieved with the relation Degrees=Radians*180/Pi, where Pi=3.141592654.

SIN(X), COS(X) and TAN(X):
The sine, cosine and tangent functions require an argument angle expressed in radians. If the angle is stated in degrees, then use the relation Radians=Degrees*Pi/180.

SQR(X):
The SQR() function returns the square root of the number supplied to it.

To illustrate the use of the above functions, consider a simple problem involving a 2 m long ladder resting against a wall with the angle between ladder and ground being 60 degrees. With the help of simple trigonometry we shall work out the vertical distance between the top of the ladder and the ground, the horizontal distance between the foot of the ladder and the wall and also the ratio of the vertical to horizontal distance.

The program uses the trigonometric functions SIN(), COS(), TAN(), ATAN() and the SQR() function to solve the problem. It then calculates the original angle and ladder length.

```
REM LADDER AGAINST WALL
Pi=3.141592654
Angle=60:REM IN DEGREES
Arads=Angle*Pi/180:REM IN RADIANS
Vert=2*SIN(Arads)
Horiz=2*COS(Arads)
Ratio=TAN(Arads)
PRINT "ORIG ANGLE =";Angle
PRINT "VERT DIST =";Vert
PRINT "HORIZ DIST =";Horiz
PRINT "RATIO =";Ratio
Arads2=ATN(Vert/Horiz)
Angle2=Arads2*180/Pi
PRINT "CALC ANGLE =";Angle2
Length=SQR(Vert^2 + Horiz^2)
PRINT "CALC LADDER LENGTH =";Length
END
```

On **Run**ning the program, Basic will respond with

```
ORIG ANGLE = 60
VERT DIST = 1.732051
HORIZ DIST = .9999999
```

```
RATIO = 1.732051
CALC ANGLE = 60
CALC LADDER LENGTH = 2
```

ABS(X):

The ABS() function returns the absolute (that is, positive) value of a given number. For example ABS(1.234) is 1.234, while ABS(–2.345) is returned as 2.345.

The ABS() function can be used to detect whether the values of two variables say, X and Y, are within an acceptable limit by using the statement in the form

```
IF ABS(X-Y) < 0.0001) THEN
```

in which case the block of statements following the THEN will be executed only if the absolute difference of the two variables is less than the specified limit, indicating that they are approximately equal. We need to use the ABS() function in the above statement otherwise a negative difference, no matter how small, would be less than the specified small positive number.

Problem 5.1

Newton's method of finding the square root of a number x is as follows:

(a) Make a guess at the square root, say q. A good approximation for this could be built into the program as q = x/2.

(b) Find r = x/q

(c) Find the average of r and q

(d) If r is approximately equal to q (use the absolute function in the statement IF ABS(r–q) < 0.001), then the average in (c) gives a good approximation of the square root

(e) Otherwise, take the average as the new value of q and repeat from (b).

Write a program capable of finding the square root of any number.

EXP(X):
The exponential function raises the number e to the power of X. The EXP() function is the inverse of the LOG() function. The relationship is

LOG(EXP(X)) = X

LOG(X):
The logarithm to base e is given by the above function. Logarithms to the base e may easily be converted to any other base using the identity

$log_a(N)$ = LOG(N)/LOG(a)

where $log_a(N)$ stands for the desired logarithm to base a, while LOG(N) and LOG(a) stand for the logarithm to the base e of N and a, respectively.

Antilogarithm functions are not given but they can easily be derived using the following identities:

Antilog(X)=e^X (base e; this is EXP(X))
Antilog(X)=10^X (base 10)

INT(X):
The integer function returns the value of X rounded down to the nearest integer. Thus, INT(6.97) returns the value 6, whilst INT(-6.789) returns the value -7.

Numbers can be rounded to the nearest whole number, rather than rounding down, by using the function INT(X+0.5). For example, INT(5.67+0.5) returns the value 6. It can also be used to round to any given number of decimal places, or to the nearest integer power of 10, by using the expression:

INT(X*10^D+0.5)/10^D

where D is (a) a positive integer or (b) a negative integer supplied by the user. For rounding to the first decimal, D=1; to the nearest 100, D=-2. The program given on the next page will help to illustrate these points.

```
REM ROUNDING NUMBERS
DO
    INPUT "ENTER A NUMBER ", X#
    IF X#=0 THEN END
    INPUT "HOW MANY DEC PLACES "; D%
    N#=INT(X#*10^D%+0.5)/10^D%
    PRINT N#:PRINT
LOOP UNTIL False
```

Type the program into your computer and **Run** it. Results of a typical run are given below:

```
ENTER A NUMBER 1.23456
HOW MANY DEC PLACES ? 3
1.235

ENTER A NUMBER 25.6789
HOW MANY DEC PLACES ? 2
25.68

ENTER A NUMBER 120.5
HOW MANY DEC PLACES ? -2
100
```

Try it yourself. To stop the program enter 0 (zero).

SGN(X):
The sign function returns 1 if X is positive, 0 if X=0, and −1 if X is negative.

RND and RANDOMIZE n:
The RND function is used to produce a pseudo randomly selected number from 0 to 1, but which does not include 1. The RANDOMIZE function allows the random-number generator RND to start from a 'seed number' and produce a series of numbers based on the seed. By using the same seed again, the same series of numbers can be obtained. The statement RANDOMIZE, by itself, requests a 'Random Number Seed', while RANDOMIZE n seeds the random number generator RND with the number that n represents. The statement RANDOMIZE TIMER uses the computer's internal clock to seed the random-number generator RND.

Random numbers are used in statistical programs and in all kinds of simulations from simple games to complex computer models. In some programs, especially business simulations, it is necessary to reproduce the same 'random' conditions from run to run. This is done with the dice throwing program given below. Type the program and **Run** it.

```
REM THROWING DICE
FOR J=1 TO 2
    RANDOMIZE 2
    PRINT TAB(7); "THROW    NUMBER"
    FOR I=1 TO 6: PRINT TAB(6); I, RND: NEXT I
NEXT J
END
```

The program produces the same random throws as shown over the page. Note that both sets of throws produce the same numbers because of the position and the type of the RANDOMIZE statement.

```
THROW        NUMBER
1            1.414126E-02
2            .6076428
3            .3568624
4            .9575312
5            .2980418
6            .7864588
THROW        NUMBER
1            1.414126E-02
2            .6076428
3            .3568624
4            .9575312
5            .2980418
6            .7864588
```

In some contexts it is a severe disadvantage to have the same series of random numbers produced. To overcome this problem, you must set the seed to a random value. First change the seed from 2 to J by using the statement

```
RANDOMIZE J
```

and **Run** the program again.

You will now notice that the random numbers resulting from the first set of dice throws are different from the ones given above, namely

THROW	NUMBER
1	.7648737
2	.1054455
3	.6134542
4	.9377558
5	.1073679
6	.1084803

but the second set is identical to the previous results. When the program is run again, the same set of random numbers are reproduced, because the seed is the same. If you change the random number seed to the value of the internal clock with the statement

```
RANDOMIZE TIMER
```

not only the two sets of random numbers (corresponding to the two sets of dice throws) will be different, but also different sets of random numbers will result each time the program is run, as the seed would have changed.

Derived Mathematical Functions

Some useful mathematical functions which can be derived from standard Basic functions are listed below:

Derived Mathematical Functions

Function	*Formula*
TRIGONOMETRIC	
Cosecant	CSC(X)=1/SIN(X)
Cotangent	COT(X)=1/TAN(X)
Secant	SEC(X)=1/COS(X)
INVERSE TRIGONOMETRIC	
Arc Cosine	ACOS(X)=–ATN(X/SQR(–X*X+1))+Pi/2
Arc Sine	ASIN(X)=ATN(X/SQR(–X*X+1))
Arc Cosecant	ACSC(X)=ATN(1/SQR(X*X–1))+(SGN(X)–1)*Pi/2
Arc Cotangent	ACOT(X)=–ATN(X)+Pi/2
Arc Secant	ASEC(X)=ATN(SQR(X*X–1))+(SGN(X)–1)*Pi/2

HYPERBOLIC

Hyp Cosine	COSH(X)=(EXP(X)+EXP(-X))/2
Hyp Sine	SINH(X)=(EXP(X)-EXP(-X))/2
Hyp Tangent	TANH(X)=-EXP(-X)/(EXP(X)+EXP(-X))*2+1
Hyp Cosecant	CSCH(X)=2/(EXP(X)-EXP(-X))
Hyp Cotangent	COTH(X)=EXP(-X)/(EXP(X)-EXP(-X))*2+1
Hyp Secant	SECH(X)=2/(EXP(X)+EXP(-X))

INVERSE HYPERBOLIC

Arc Cosh	ACOSH(X)=LOG(X+SQR(X*X-1))
Arc Sinh	ASINH(X)=LOG(X+SQR(X*X+1))
Arc Tanh	ATANH(X)=LOG((1+X)/(1-X))/2
Arc Cosech	ACSCH(X)=LOG((SGN(X)*SQR(X*X+1)+1)/X)
Arc Cotanh	ACOTH(X)=LOG((X+1)/(X-1))/2
Arc Sech	ASECH(X)=LOG((SQR(-X*X+1)+1)/X)

Note: The constant Pi in the above formulae has the value of 3.141592654.

User-Defined Functions

In some programs it may be necessary to use the same mathematical expression in several places, often using different data. Basic user-defined functions enable definition of unique operations or expressions. These can then be called in the same manner as standard functions.

The user-defined function is identified by a special call name followed by a parenthesised argument. The first two letters of the function name must be FN, while the rest of the letters may be any legitimate variable name. Such a function however, must be defined using the DEF statement which must be placed at the beginning of a program, prior to its use by the main program. Multi-line DEF FN-type definitions of user-defined functions are also possible, but again they must be placed at the beginning of a program. The following program illustrates the use of a single-line user-defined function.

```
REM SINGLE-LINE USER-DEFINED FUNCTION
REM AREA OF A CIRCLE
Pi=3.141592654
DEF FNArea(R)=Pi*R^2
```

```
FOR I=1 TO 10
    A=FNArea(I)
    PRINT I, A
NEXT I
END
```

The program calculates the areas of circles with radii of integer values between 1 and 10. The formula is given in the DEF FNArea() statement of the fourth line. The value for the radius is passed to the function via a parenthesised variable known as the function 'formal parameter', 'argument' or 'dummy variable'. Note that the variable name representing this parameter in the definition of the function need not be the same as that used in the calling statement within the main body of the program. When called, the parenthesised argument may be any legal expression; its value is simply substituted for the function variable.

The program below, which calculates the volume of a cylinder, is used to illustrate multi-line DEF FN-type user-defined functions. Save it under the filename DEFVOL.

```
REM MULTI-LINE DEF FN-TYPE USER-DEFINED FUNCTION
REM VOLUME OF A CYLINDER
DEF FNVolume(R,H)
Pi=3.141592654
Barea=Pi*R^2
FNVolume=Barea*H
END DEF
INPUT "RADIUS OF CYLINDER "; Radius
INPUT "HEIGHT OF CYLINDER "; Height
PRINT "VOLUME="; FNVolume(Radius,Height)
END
```

The function is defined prior to its use by the main program, and two parameters are passed to it; Radius and Height. The actual parameters and the numbers held in them are passed to the two formal parameters R and H.

Further, we have calculated the base area (Barea) of the cylinder separately in order to demonstrate local and shared (or global) variables.

The symbols parenthesised in the DEF line, called formal parameters (such as R and H in the first line of the function definition), are local variables which means that their value is only known to the function.

All other variables are called shared or global variables, which means that their values are known to both the function and the main program. In order to illustrate this last point, add the following line to the above program prior to the END statement:

```
PRINT Pi, Barea
```

and **Run** it. You will see that the values held in Pi and Barea are accessible from the main program even though these values were assigned in the function after the call to it from the main program.

Procedures

QuickBASIC supports two kinds of procedures; user-defined functions and subprograms. A user-defined function which is defined as a procedure is far more powerful than the DEF FN-type declaration which must be part of the main program. Similarly, a subprogram is a modular and separate part of a program and differs from a subroutine which is part of the main program and requires the statements GOSUB and RETURN.

Procedures are blocks of program code which are isolated from the main program. QuickBASIC maintains procedures as distinct entities which can be individually tested and debugged. All variables used in procedures are local to that procedure and can not be confused with those of the main program, even if they happen to have the same names. In contrast, variables in user-defined functions of the DEF FN-type and subroutines, are global to the whole program.

To illustrate how we can use the QuickBASIC editor to write a procedure, we will use the previous program saved under the filename DEFVOL. If you have not saved this program, then type in the few lines listed overleaf, otherwise load it, delete the first line and all lines between DEF FNVolume and END DEF, and change the name of the function in the main program from FNVolume to Volume. The resulting program should look as follows:

```
REM VOLUME OF A CYLINDER
INPUT "RADIUS OF CYLINDER "; Radius
INPUT "HEIGHT OF CYLINDER "; Height
PRINT "VOLUME="; Volume(Radius,Height)
END
```

Having the above lines in the view window, use **Alt+E** to invoke the **E**dit sub-menu and select the New **F**unction option. At this point a dialogue window will open and you will be asked to type the name of the function. Typing Volume and pressing <Enter>, causes the screen to clear and the following two lines to be displayed

```
FUNCTION Volume _
END FUNCTION
```

with the cursor appearing at the end of the first line. You can now type in the parameter list and the rest of the function statements, as follows:

```
FUNCTION Volume(R,H)
    Pi=3.141592654
    Barea=Pi*R^2
    Volume=Barea*H
END FUNCTION
```

Pressing the **F2** function key allows you to choose which portion of your program (main part or procedure) to edit. Pressing **F5** from any module runs the program.

Save this program under the filename VOLUME. On executing the **S**ave command, you will notice that QuickBASIC adds automatically the line

```
DECLARE FUNCTION Volume!(R!,H!)
```

as the first line of your main program. When you reload the program later, this line is part of the main program listing. Whether this line has been added by QuickBASIC or it was typed in because we intend to use already written procedures with the main program, such declarations will be shown in all appropriate program listings, from this point on in the book.

Procedures, such as user-defined functions discussed above, or subprograms to be discussed shortly, are self-contained program units which can perform specific functions. They can be called from any part of the main program.

After a procedure has been executed, program control is returned to the statement following the calling statement. It is, therefore, possible to build up a library of standard procedures, which can then be invoked from a main program to solve large and complex problems.

Unlike user-defined functions of the DEF FN-type which can not be passed information regarding an array, procedures can be passed entire arrays by including the array name in the parameter list. You must not, however, DIMension such an array within the procedure.

Problem 5.2

Modify the program given above so that it incorporates a second user-defined function which rounds, to the second decimal place, the calculated values for the volumes. Use the formula given under the INT() function with a value for D = 2.

Subprograms

Subprograms are in many ways similar to user-defined procedure functions. However, the major difference between them is that, whereas functions return a single value to the main program via their name, subprograms can be used to pass many values to the main program through variables in the parameter list.

The general form of a subprogram which could be used to, say, calculate the sum of money returned on an investment, is written as follows:

```
SUB Interest(Principal, Rate, Years)
    ---
    ---
END SUB
```

To call this procedure from any part of the main program, including from within the subprogram itself, we must use the following call statement

```
CALL Interest(P, R, Y)
```

where variables P, R and Y are the actual parameters.

After all the statements in a subprogram are executed or an EXIT SUB statement is encountered, program control reverts to the statement that follows the CALL statement in the main program.

Fig. 5.1 shows in diagrammatic form the flow of program control, when a subprogram is used. When the CALL Proc_X statement is encountered in the main body of the program, it causes a jump to the first statement of the subprogram, SUB Proc_X, and continues to execute the statements within it until the END SUB statement is met which diverts program control to the statement immediately following the call statement.

Successive call statements can branch to the same subprogram. Each time the END SUB statement is reached, the main program is resumed at the last call statement from which it branched.

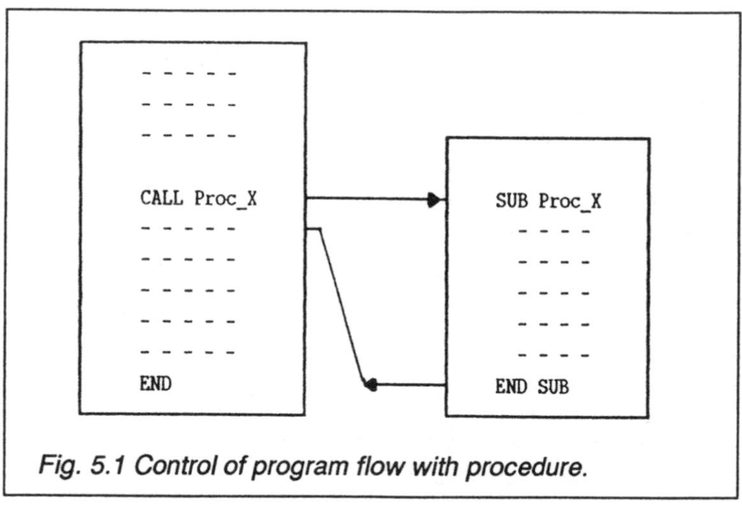

Fig. 5.1 Control of program flow with procedure.

The following program, which calculates the compound interest on money lent (see solution to Problem 3.2), will be used to illustrate the use of subprograms. The program calculates the compound interest using the formula

```
A = P * (1+Rate/100)^Years
```

where P is the principal (original) money lent, and A is what it amounts to in time Years at Rate per cent per annum.

```
DECLARE SUB Interest(Principal!,Rate!,N%,Amount!)
REM COMPOUND INTEREST
DEFINT N, Y
INPUT "Enter original money lent ", Original
INPUT "Enter interest rate ", Rate
INPUT "Enter No. of years ", Years
PRINT SPC(1); "YEAR"; SPC(12); "AMOUNT"
FOR N=1 TO Years
    CALL Interest(Original, Rate, N, Amount)
    Form$="#####     ####,###.##"
    PRINT USING Form$; N, Amount
NEXT N
END
DEFINT N, Y
SUB Interest(Principal, Rate, N, Amount)
    Amount=Principal*(1+Rate/100)^N
END SUB
```

After entering the investment parameters Original, Rate and Years, the subprogram Interest is called several times from within the FOR...NEXT loop set up in the main part of the program. The parameters are passed to it at the same time through the argument list of the call statement. The values of these parameters are then used as the variables Principal, Rate, and N in the subprogram. After executing all the statements within the subprogram, program control passes back to the line following the CALL statement in the main program, where the string Form$ is being set up for use with the PRINT USING statement which follows, in order to print the results of each iteration of the loop (held in variable Amount), correctly formatted.

Save the program under the filename COMPINT and **Run** it using the values shown below for the three variables.

```
Enter original money lent 5000
Enter interest rate 11
Enter No. of years 15
```

The program then proceeds to calculate the compound interest on the money lent, and displays the results as follows:

YEARS	AMOUNT
1	5,550.00
2	6,160.50
3	6,838.15
4	7,590.35
5	8,425.29
6	9,352.07
7	10,380.80
8	11,522.69
9	12,790.18
10	14,197.10
11	15,758.79
12	17,492.25
13	19,416.40
14	21,552.21
15	23,922.95

Note that when a procedure is created, QuickBASIC assumes that DEFinition instructions relating to the type of variables used in the main part of the program (DEFINT N,Y in the previous example) also apply to the procedure. Thus, when QuickBASIC opens a window for a new procedure, the active type definition instructions appear above the FUNCTION or SUB statement. These can be edited, but be careful as active type definition instructions control the default data type for formal parameters.

Problem 5.3

Modify the solution to Problem 5.2 by making function Volume into a subprogram from within which function Round is called. Use the variable Result within the argument list of the subprogram CALL statement and Res as the formal parameter in the subprogram definition.

Differences Between Functions and Subprograms:

All the tasks that are performed by procedure-type functions can also be performed by subprograms. There are, however, two main differences between the two. These are listed below:

(1) Functions are invoked by simply using their name in an expression, while subprograms are invoked by using the CALL statement.

(2) A function name not only identifies the function, but also is used to assign a value to it by the statements within its definition. This value can be a string, or any of the four numeric types. A subprogram name, on the other hand, only serves to identify the subprogram and has no value.

Parameter Passing

There are two fundamental rules relating to parameter passing. These are: (a) the number of arguments in an argument list of the call statement must be the same as that of the formal parameters, and (b) the data type of each argument must match the data type of the corresponding formal parameter.

The formal parameters in a procedure, whether a subprogram or function, are variable names local to that particular procedure. The actual parameter passed to the procedure can either be (i) a variable name local to the calling program or (ii) a literal, constant, or expression.

In the first case, when a parameter is a variable, parameter passing is by 'reference', which means that the address of the variable is passed to the procedure. As the formal parameter within the procedure is also assigned to the same address, this means that any changes to the formal parameter within the procedure can be passed back to the main program.

In the second case, when a parameter is a literal, constant, or an expression, parameter passing is by 'value', which means that the actual value is passed rather than the address in which the value is held. In this case, the value of an expression is calculated, the result is stored in a temporary location and the address of the temporary location is passed to the procedure. As a result, any changes to this parameter by the procedure is only reflected in the temporary address and the original value accessed by the main program remains unmodified.

Variables within functions of the DEF FN-type, which are supported by QuickBASIC so that compatibility with BASICA can be maintained, are global to the main program. To declare variables local use the STATIC declaration. All arguments are passed by value.

To pass a variable by value in procedures, enclose the variable name in parentheses. This makes the argument into an expression which has the desired effect. A function of the DEF FN-type can only pass parameters by value.

The short programs given below will help to illustrate the points made above. First, the program

```
DECLARE SUB Count(K!)
REM PASS-BY-REFERENCE
K=0
CALL Count(K)
PRINT K
END
SUB Count(K)
     K=K+1
     PRINT K,
END SUB
```

when **Run**, will display

```
1              1
```

while the program

```
REM PASS-BY-VALUE
DEF FNCount(K)
     K=K+1
     FNCount=K
END DEF
K=0
PRINT FNCount(K),K
END
```

when **Run**, will display

```
1              0
```

As a consequence of this pass-by-value rule, an array can not be passed to a function of the DEF FN-type, while as a consequence of the pass-by-reference rule, an entire array can be passed to a procedure.

Procedures can be made to pass-by-value by enclosing the variable name with an extra pair of brackets in the call statement. For example, using

```
CALL Count((K))
```

in the subprogram, will give the same output as the DEF FN-type function program.

Passing Arrays to Procedures:
To pass an entire array to a procedure the actual name of the array being passed, followed by an empty pair of parentheses, must be included as a parameter in the argument list of the call statement. In the SUB statement of the procedure definition, the formal name for the array being used must appear as a parameter in the argument list followed by a pair of parentheses that contain the number of dimensions of the array. To illustrate the above points, the BUBBLE SORT program discussed in the previous chapter is written with a procedure, as shown below:

```
DECLARE SUB Rotate (Employee$(), I!, Flag!)
REM BUBBLE SORT
READ N:DIM Employee$(N)
FOR I=1 TO N: READ Employee$(I): NEXT I
FOR I=1 TO N: PRINT Employee$(I): NEXT I
PRINT: PRINT: PRINT "SORTED INFORMATION"
M=N
FOR J=1 TO N-1
    M=M-1: Flag=0
    FOR I=1 TO M
     IF Employee$(I)>Employee$(I+1) THEN
       CALL Rotate(Employee$(), I, Flag)
     END IF
    NEXT I
    IF Flag=0 THEN EXIT FOR
NEXT J
FOR I=1 TO N: PRINT Employee$(I): NEXT I
END
DATA 5
DATA "WILSON M.  ,ROOM 1.24 ,  395"
DATA "SMITH M.   ,ROOM 2.6  ,7315"
DATA "JONES B.M. ,ROOM 6.19 ,1698"
DATA "SMITH A.A. ,ROOM 2.12 ,  456"
DATA "BROWN C.   ,ROOM 3.1  ,  432"
SUB Rotate(Employee$(1), I, Flag)
    Flag=1
    Temp$=Employee$(I+1)
    Employee$(I+1)=Employee$(I)
    Employee$(I)=Temp$
END SUB
```

The program prints only the original and sorted data. The Rotate procedure can be made shorter and faster by using the QuickBASIC SWAP statement, as follows:

```
SWAP Employee$(I+1), Employee$(I)
```

in place of the three lines following the Flag=1 line. Do this last change and **S**ave the program as PROCSORT.

Declaring Arrays within Functions and Procedures:
Both functions of the DEF FN-type, and procedures can use arrays within their block definitions even though only procedures can have arrays passed to them.

To use an array within a function of the DEF FN-type which you want to be local to the function, you must declare it as STATIC. In declaring an array in this way, the name of the array followed by an empty pair of parentheses must appear in the declaration. Following this, the array must be dimensioned in an appropriate DIM statement within the function definition, as follows:

```
DEF FNExample
     STATIC Array()
     DIM Array(15)
     - - -
END DEF
```

The general format of the STATIC instruction is:

STATIC Variable_name AS *type*

where Variable_name is a simple variable name or an array name followed by empty parentheses (), and *type* specifies the variable's data type which can be INTEGER, LONG, SINGLE, DOUBLE, STRING or user-defined (record) type.

The STATIC instruction can effect a variable in two ways: (a) it turns a global variable local to the user-defined function or procedure, (b) makes the variable static - that is it preserves its original value between successive calls to the procedure.

In procedures arrays declared within the procedure itself will be local to that procedure. However, it is possible to make such an array a shared array with the main program by the use of the SHARED statement.

The SHARED Statement:
The SHARED statement can be used whenever we would like to make a certain variable or an array of a procedure global to the main program. The general format of the instruction is:

```
SHARED Variable_name AS type
```

where Variable_name can be a simple variable name or an array name followed by empty parentheses, and *type* specifies the variable's data type which can be INTEGER, LONG, SINGLE, DOUBLE, STRING or user-defined (record) type.

The SHARED instruction is only valid within a user-defined function or subprogram, not in the main program.

If you want to make a variable global to all procedures, then use the SHARED keyword in a DIM statement within the main program, as follows:

```
DIM SHARED Variable_name
```

where Variable_name can be a simple variable or an array name followed by empty parentheses.

If you want to share variables between multiple modules, then use the COMMON statement.

The COMMON Statement:
The COMMON statement collects a group of variables into a COMMON block. By declaring the same COMMON block in different modules, you can make the variables global between the various modules. The general format of the instruction is:

```
COMMON [SHARED] [/Block_name/] Variable_list
```

where Block_name is the name of the COMMON block, and Variable_list is a list of variable names, separated by a comma, placed in the COMMON block. Instructions appearing in square brackets are optional.

If Block_name is specified, then the block is known as a 'named' COMMON. If, on the other hand, Block_name is not specified, the block is known as a 'blank' COMMON.

Variable_list consists of simple variable names or array names followed by empty parentheses. The data type of each variable can be specified with a type-declaration suffix or an AS type clause, in the same way as SHARED and STATIC variable declarations.

The COMMON statement must appear before any executable statement in a module. When an array is inserted into a COMMON block, the DIM statement for that array must appear before the COMMON statement.

Recursion

Not only can a function or procedure invoke other functions and/or procedures, but it can also invoke itself. This process is called 'recursion'. Recursion can lead to some very elegant and efficient programs. The program listed below can be used to provide a conversion table from one currency to another. It is recursive, with the procedure calling itself many times until the problem is completed. This program is worth studying as recursive programming can be a very powerful technique once it is understood.

```
DECLARE SUB Conversion(Rate!, Max!)
REM CURRENCY CONVERSION (RECURSIVE)
INPUT "CURRENCY 1 "; Currency1$
INPUT "CURRENCY 2 "; Currency2$
INPUT "EXCHANGE RATE? "; Rate
INPUT "MAXIMUM RANGE? "; Max
PRINT: PRINT Currency1$, Currency2$
CALL Conversion(Rate, Max)
END
SUB Conversion(Rate, Max)
    IF Max<1 THEN EXIT SUB
    CALL Conversion(Rate, Max-1)
     Form$="######  ####,###.##"
     PRINT USING Form$; Max; Max*Rate
END SUB
```

Save the program under the filename RECURS. On **Run**ning it Basic asks you to define CURRENCY 1 and CURRENCY 2, the EXCHANGE RATE and the MAXIMUM RANGE. On supplying the information shown below

```
CURRENCY 1 ? Pounds
CURRENCY 2 ? Dollars
EXCHANGE RATE ? 1.54
MAXIMUM RANGE ? 10
```

Basic calculates and PRINTs the answers as follows:

Pounds	Dollars
1	1.54
2	3.08
3	4.62
4	6.16
5	7.70
6	9.24
7	10.78
8	12.32
9	13.86
10	15.40

It is quite difficult to understand how the logic of a recursive procedure works at first. To illustrate the process, we shall look at the above example with Max=3. Fig. 5.2 shows the logic flow. Remember that program control returns to the statement after the last procedure CALL when an END SUB statement is reached.

If we hadn't used recursion, we would have had to set up a loop to iterate through the range 1-10. By using recursion, we have broken the problem down into several simpler ones of printing up to the value of Max–1. This is repeated until Max–1 is less than one.

After the first CALL statement the program diverts to the procedure with Max set to 3. As Max is not less than 1, program control passes to the second CALL statement with Max=2. Once more control is passed to the third CALL statement with Max=1. Finally, this is repeated with Max=0. At this point a change in the program flow takes place because Max is less than 1 so the last EXIT SUB is executed. The last Form$ line is then reached and the first line of the table is printed. The last END SUB is now executed, so the program jumps to the line following the previous procedure call and the second line of the table is printed. This is repeated once more before control passes to the END statement where program execution halts.

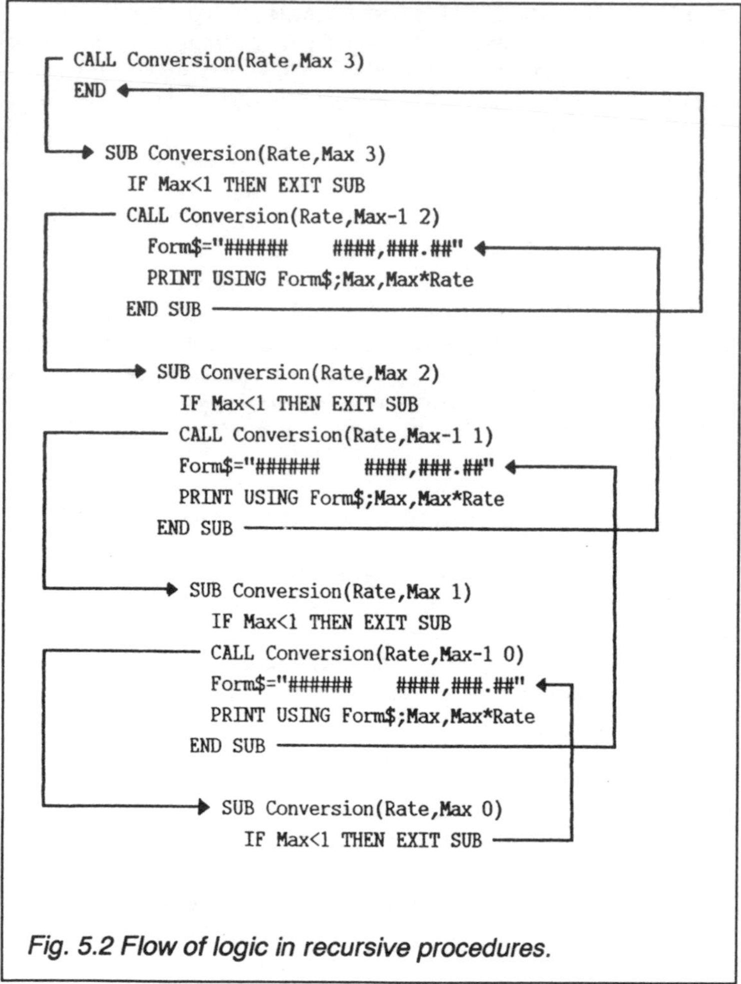
CALL Conversion(Rate,Max 3)
END
SUB Conversion(Rate,Max 3)
IF Max<1 THEN EXIT SUB
CALL Conversion(Rate,Max-1 2)
Form$="######   ####,###.##"
PRINT USING Form$;Max,Max*Rate
END SUB
SUB Conversion(Rate,Max 2)
IF Max<1 THEN EXIT SUB
CALL Conversion(Rate,Max-1 1)
Form$="######   ####,###.##"
PRINT USING Form$;Max,Max*Rate
END SUB
SUB Conversion(Rate,Max 1)
IF Max<1 THEN EXIT SUB
CALL Conversion(Rate,Max-1 0)
Form$="######   ####,###.##"
PRINT USING Form$;Max,Max*Rate
END SUB
SUB Conversion(Rate,Max 0)
IF Max<1 THEN EXIT SUB

Fig. 5.2 Flow of logic in recursive procedures.

Subroutines

Subroutines are similar to procedures in many ways but they are not as powerful. They are supported by QuickBASIC primarily because they are the only way that standard BASIC can code frequently used sections of logic into subprograms. Thus, programs written for standard BASIC can be easily adapted to run under QuickBASIC.

The GOSUB and RETURN Statements:
When Basic encounters the GOSUB statement in the main body of the program, it branches to the first statement of the subroutine, and continues to execute the statements within the subroutine until the RETURN statement is encountered. This diverts program flow to the statement immediately following the GOSUB statement which called the subroutine. Thus, the GOSUB statement broadly corresponds to the CALL statement, while the RETURN corresponds to the END SUB.

When successive GOSUB statements branch to the same subroutine, each time the RETURN statement is reached, the main program is resumed at the last GOSUB statement from which it branched. No line reference is necessary. We shall now modify the COMPINT program which we used to demonstrate procedures in order to illustrate subroutines. The modified program is shown below:

```
REM COMPOUND INTEREST (WITH SUBROUTINE)
DEFINT N,Y
INPUT "Enter original money lent ", Original
INPUT "Enter interest rate ", Rate
INPUT "Enter No. of years ", Years
PRINT:PRINT SPC(1); "YEAR"; SPC(12); "AMOUNT"
FOR N=1 TO Years
     Principal=Original
     GOSUB Interest
     Form$="#####     ####,###.##"
     PRINT USING Form$; N, Amount
NEXT N: PRINT
END
REM SUBROUTINE TO CALCULATE COMPOUND INTEREST
Interest:
     Amount=Principal*(1+Rate/100)^N
RETURN
```

After entering the investment parameters Original, Rate and Years, the subroutine is called several times from within the FOR...NEXT loop set up in the main part of the program. The parameter Principal, required within the subroutine, is initialised by the statement in the line preceding the GOSUB statement. Subroutines cannot have local variables, therefore, all variables are equivalent to SHARED variables in procedures.

After executing all the statements within the subroutine, program control passes back to the statement following the GOSUB in the main program (the Form$ statement). **S**ave this program under the filename COMPSUB, and then **Run** it to verify that you get the same results as before.

Exercises

1. Three truck sizes are available to move a given volume of earth. Write a program to calculate the number of truck loads of each size required, using the following logic.

   (a) The large trucks must be used first, if possible, as long as they are full,
   (b) the medium size trucks should be used next, as long as they are full,
   (c) the smallest trucks should take the remaining load, if any.

   The information to be processed by your program is as follows:

   (i) Volume of ore to be moved,
   (ii) capacity (in volume) of the largest truck,
   (iii) capacity (in volume) of the middle-sized truck,
   (iv) capacity (in volume) of the smallest truck.

   Your program should accept data consisting of these four values and with the use of the INT() function should evaluate the number of trucks required and produce the following tabulated output.

   Volume of earth to be moved = ******

	Large Capac = *****	Medium Capac = ****	Small Capac = ***
No. of full trucks	***	****	*****
No. of part full trucks			***

   Note that only small sized trucks could be part full.

2. Write a program which reads the coefficients A, B and C of a quadratic equation, i.e.

$$Ax^2 + Bx + C = 0$$

and uses the formula

$$x = \frac{-B \pm \sqrt{\{B^2 - 4AC\}}}{2A}$$

to solve for the two roots of the equation. The program must test whether A=0, as well as whether $\{B^2 - 4AC\}$ is equal, greater or less than zero. If $\{B^2 - 4AC\}$ is negative, then the two roots of the equation are deemed to be complex in which case the real (–B/2A) and the imaginary ($\pm\{B^2 - 4AC\}/2A$) parts of each root must be given separately.

Test your program with the following data:

A	B	C
1	–10	25
0	–2	1
0.02	–0.04	0.02
1	2	5
1	0	–1
1	0	1
1	2	1

3. Two points A and B have coordinates given by (x_1,y_1) and x_2,y_2 respectively. Write a program to calculate the distance of separation between the points given by

$$\sqrt{\{(y_2-y_1)^2 + (x_2-x_1)^2\}}$$

However, instead of using the internal function SQR(), use the program given as the solution to Problem 5.1, suitably adapted to a function subprogram to evaluate the square root.

4. Rewrite the solution to Problem 3.3 (The three number sort) suitably modified as a procedure with the three parameters A, B and C in its argument list. Then write a main program that reads the lengths of the three sides of a triangle and calls the procedure to sort their values in ascending order so that variable C holds the largest of the three. Then use the identity

$$C^2 = A^2 + B^2$$

to test whether the three sides form a right triangle or not.

For non-integer values for A, B and C you will find that it is necessary to use the ABS() function in order to test whether $A^2 + B^2$ is approximately equal to C^2.

6. DISC FILING SYSTEM

Programs can be stored on disc quite easily. Just as easily, we can use a disc to store data in files called 'data files'. We will identify them by saving them on disc under filenames with .DAT extensions. Three types of data files can be used to store information, namely sequential, random access or binary files. Each type has advantages and disadvantages. Sequential files use disc space efficiently, but are difficult to update a single piece of information within their structure. Random files are less efficient as far as usage of disc space is concerned, but provide quick access to information. Binary files offer great flexibility, but have no structure and, therefore, are difficult to program. We shall investigate these, by first looking at their individual structure and then by discussing how data can be written to, and read from, each type of file.

Sequential Data Files

A sequential data file can be thought of as a one dimensional array with each array location being one byte, capable of holding one character of a string. For example, the name of a friend together with his telephone number

ADAMS M. 02-1893

could be stored as shown below:

```
Byte                     1                   2
      0 1 2 3 4 5 6 7 8 9 0 1 2 3 4 5 6 7 8 9 0 1
Char  " A D A M S   M . " , " 0 2 - 1 8 9 3 " ¶ ⇓
```

Of special importance to sequential data files are the three ASCII control characters 10 (linefeed – LF), 13 (carriage return – CR), both shown by the symbol ¶, and 26 (End-of-File marker – EOF), shown above as ⇓. The combination CR/LF (¶) is issued every time you press the <Enter> key.

Two friends' names will be stored with the second name following the first, separated by LF/CR, with the EOF character marking the end of file. For example,

```
"ADAMS M.","02-1893"¶"SIMS I.","01-1351"¶⇓
```

Carriage returns/linefeeds (¶) mark the end of blocks of information called 'records' with each record containing related information such as names and telephone numbers separated by commas, called 'fields'. Fields can hold anyone of the five different types of variables, such as strings (which appear in quotation marks), integers, long integers, single- and/or double-precision variables.

To write data into a sequential data file we must write a small Basic program which will 'create' such a file and then 'write' into it the characters representing the information we would like to store on disc. The strings which make up each field of the file will first be READ into the computer and stored in an appropriate string array, and subsequently transferred onto the disc. The program below does this.

```
REM CREATE A SEQ. DATA FILE
READ New: DIM Aname$(New), Tel$(New)
FOR I=1 TO New: READ Aname$(I), Tel$(I): NEXT I
DATA 2
DATA "ADAMS M.", "02-1893"
DATA "SIMS I.", "01-1351"
INPUT "NAME TO SAVE UNDER? ", Filename$
OPEN Filename$+".DAT" FOR OUTPUT AS #1
FOR I=1 TO New: WRITE #1,  Aname$(I), Tel$(I): NEXT I
CLOSE #1
OPEN Filename$+".IDX" FOR OUTPUT AS #2
WRITE #2, New
CLOSE #2
END
```

The first two executable lines of the program allow READing of each field which is then stored in string arrays Aname$ and Tel$. Following the INPUT line, the commands OPEN Filename$ FOR OUTPUT AS #1, WRITE #1 and CLOSE #1 are directed to the filing system. The first OPENs a specified file with the extension .DAT for OUTPUT, through the communications channel #1. By OPENing a file, the name of that file is automatically written on the directory of the logged drive. If the filename already exists, the OPEN command will delete its contents, which means that you lose all the information already stored in that file.

The first WRITE command within the FOR...NEXT loop, writes to the file with the extension .DAT the actual data held in string arrays Aname$ and Tel$. When all the data has been written to the file, the file is then CLOSEd.

Following this, the program creates another file, by the same name but with extension .IDX, in which the variable New is written. The value of New gives the total number of records we have written into the data file which is sometimes useful to know.

Note the special way of writing QuickBASIC commands which are directed to the filing system. They all end with the character # followed by the channel number n (with values between 1 and 15) through which we communicate with the file. Finally, when we finish with a file we close the communications channel by the use of the CLOSE #n command.

Type this program into your computer, **S**ave it under the filename SEQUEN (which stands for 'SEQUENtial' and **Run** it. When you are asked for a file name under which to save the information, type PHONE. On completion of this program, files PHONE.DAT and PHONE.IDX are written on the directory of the logged drive and path. Make sure you give full information on the drive and directory on which you want the two files to be created.

Once data files have been created, we must be in a position to READ each field back into the computer so that information can be retrieved. This is achieved through the small Basic program (**S**ave it under the filename SEQUENRT (which stands for SEQUENtial ReTrieve) given below:

```
REM RETRIEVE A SEQ. DATA FILE
INPUT "FILE NAME TO LOAD? ", Filename$
OPEN Filename$+".IDX" FOR INPUT AS #3
INPUT #3, Total: DIM Aname$(Total), Tel$(Total)
CLOSE #3
OPEN Filename$+".DAT" FOR INPUT AS #4
FOR I=1 TO Total: INPUT #4, Aname$(I), Tel$(I): NEXT I
CLOSE #4
FOR I=1 TO Total: PRINT Aname$(I), Tel$(I): NEXT I
END
```

The third line OPENs a file with the extension .IDX, the name of which is held in string variable Filename$, for INPUT through channel #3. The next line reads the contents of the file using the INPUT #3 statement. The item read is the value of the Total number of records held in the file with the .DAT extension which is then OPENed and the information held in it is transferred into arrays Aname$ and Tel$ with the use of the INPUT #4 statement within the FOR...NEXT loop. Finally, the file is CLOSEd and arrays Aname$ and Tel$ are PRINTed on the screen.

The INPUT #n command must follow an OPEN FOR INPUT command for a file which is CLOSEd. Similarly, the WRITE #n command must follow an OPEN FOR OUTPUT command for a file which is CLOSEd. Attempting to either WRITE #n or INPUT #n on a file that has not been OPENed for OUTPUT or INPUT respectively, will cause the error 'Bad file number' to be generated. Attempting to read more records than are in the file will cause the 'Input past end' error message to appear on the screen. All error messages generated during run-time are listed in Appendix B.

Using the INPUT Statement to Create Data Files:

Another way to create sequential data files is to replace the READ...DATA statement of the SEQUEN program with the INPUT statement. This method is also useful for appending information to data files. Make the following changes to the SEQUEN program:

```
REM INPUT INTO A SEQ. DATA FILE
INPUT "NUMBER OF NEW ENTRIES? ", New
DIM Aname$(New), Tel$(New): I=0
DO
    I=I+1: PRINT ""; I; ">";: INPUT "" , Aname$(I), Tel$(I)
LOOP UNTIL I=New OR Aname$(I)=""
IF Aname$(I)="" THEN New=I-1
INPUT "NAME TO SAVE UNDER? ", Filename$
OPEN Filename$+".IDX" FOR OUTPUT AS #1
WRITE #1, New
CLOSE #1
OPEN Filename$+".DAT" FOR OUTPUT AS #2
FOR I=1 TO New: WRITE #2, Aname$(I), Tel$(I): NEXT I
CLOSE #2
END
```

Save this program under the file name SEQUENIN and then **Run** it.

The trailer of the LOOP UNTIL statement allows you to terminate entries at will prior to reaching the end of the DO loop by simply pressing <Enter>. In this case, the loop control counter I would be one more than the number of entries. The variable New is therefore set to I–1 prior to writing its value in the file.

Note that typing information relating to each individual field, in response to the INPUT statement, must be separated by a comma. For example, in the above example what is expected is a record that looks as follows:

```
Smith, 03-444
```

the use of the comma indicates to the INPUT statement that the first string should be entered into array Aname$, while the second should be entered into array Tel$.

Other Methods of Storing and Retrieving Data:
Information can be stored in a file and retrieved from a file by other statements than WRITE #n and INPUT #n. The statements PRINT #n and PRINT #n USING can be used to put data into a file in much the same way that PRINT and PRINT USING were used to display data on the screen. With PRINT #n, you can record numbers with leading or trailing spaces. The statement LINE INPUT #n can be used to read data from a sequential file. The statement

```
LINE INPUT #n, X$
```

reads all characters (including commas) to the next carriage return/linefeed in the file through channel n and assigns this string of characters to the variable X$. Just like the INPUT #n file statement has an equivalent INPUT keyboard statement, so does the LINE INPUT #n which takes the form

```
LINE INPUT Y$
```

which allows the user to enter any keyboard character into string Y$. The LINE INPUT #n statement is normally used to retrieve data that has been entered in a file using the PRINT #n statement.

Finally, the statement

```
X$=INPUT$(m,n)
```

reads the next m characters (including commas and carriage returns) from the file through channel n, and assigns them to the string variable X$.

Problem 6.1

Convert the SEQUENIN and SEQUENRT programs into procedures to use the LINE INPUT, PRINT #n, and LINE INPUT #n statements so that information (including a comma, used to separate name and telephone number) can be typed from the keyboard into string array Aname$, and subsequently stored into a sequential file named LIST. These changes eliminate the need for the existence of string array Tel$ which should be removed from the final program.

Appending to Sequential Data Files:
So far, we have seen how to create and retrieve sequential data files. However, files are seldom created in their entirety and it is therefore necessary to append records to existing files. The program below will OPEN FOR INPUT an existing file with the extension .IDX, will read the total number of 'old' records on the file, print its value on the screen and close the file. You are then asked for the number of 'new' records and array Aname$ is appropriately dimensioned. The DO loop is used to enter into Aname$(I) the new records which are then appended at the end of the sequential file with the extension .DAT, by opening the file for append with the statement

```
OPEN Filename$ FOR APPEND AS #n
```

Towards the end of the program, the total number of old plus new records is written into the .IDX file. The program to achieve all this is listed on the next page.

```
REM APPEND TO SEQ FILE
DO
    INPUT "APPEND TO WHICH FILE? ", Filename$
    IF Filename$="" THEN
      CLS
      SHELL "DIR A:\QBasic /W"
    END IF
LOOP UNTIL Filename$<>""
CLS
OPEN Filename$+".IDX" FOR INPUT AS #1
INPUT #1, Old: PRINT "NUMBER OF RECORDS = "; Old
CLOSE #1
INPUT "NUMBER OF NEW ENTRIES? ", New
DIM Aname$(New): I=0
DO
    I=I+1
    PRINT ""; I+Old; ">";: LINE INPUT "", Aname$(I)
LOOP UNTIL I=New OR Aname$(I)=""
IF Aname$(I)="" THEN New=I-1
Total=Old+New
OPEN Filename$+".DAT" FOR APPEND AS #2
FOR I=1 TO New: PRINT #2, Aname$(I): NEXT I
CLOSE #2
OPEN Filename$+".IDX" FOR OUTPUT AS #1
WRITE #1, Total
CLOSE #1
PRINT "Done": END
```

The first DO...LOOP UNTIL block of statements allow you to specify a file or press <Enter> to get a directory of the files on the screen in 'wide' format. This is achieved by using the QuickBASIC SHELL command which allows DOS commands to be executed - in this case to obtain a list of the files in the \QBasic subdirectory on the a: drive. Once a file has been selected, the screen is cleared (with the CLS command) and the .IDX file of the specified filename is opened in order to read the number of existing records in the file, the value of which is assigned to variable Old. From there on, the additional records are assigned to string array Aname$, and eventually appended to the .DAT file with the use of the

```
OPEN <filename> FOR APPEND AS #n
```

The Total number of records, Old plus New, is then written to the .IDX file.

Type this program into your computer and **S**ave it under the file name SEQUENAP. **Run** the program and test it by appending to file LIST which was created with the use of the program resulting from the solution to Problem 6.1.

Using the End of File Marker:

We have seen earlier that QuickBASIC puts the EOF marker at the end of a file. A useful function, EOF(n) where n is the communications channel with the file, can tell you if you have reached the end of a file when reading in data. For example, the following short program could be used to retrieve the LIST.DAT file

```
REM USING THE EOF MARKER
OPEN "A:\QBasic\LIST.DAT" FOR INPUT AS #1
DO UNTIL EOF(1)
    LINE INPUT #1, Aname$
    PRINT Aname$
LOOP
CLOSE #1
END
```

The above program assumes that file LIST.DAT is to be found in the subdirectory \QBasic in the A: drive. The DO UNTIL...LOOP block of statements is executed as long as EOF is not true. Information is read into string variable Aname$, a record at a time, and printed on the screen.

This method of reading data dispenses with the need of having to keep and index (.IDX) file in which to keep information regarding the number of records to be found in the data file under question. However, since we don't know the number of records in the file, we cannot dimension accurately a string array in order to read all the records into it. We could, of course, OPEN the file, read and count all the records and then use the information to dimension the required array. For example, the program on the next page will do this.

```
REM USING THE EOF MARKER
OPEN "A:\QBasic\LIST.DAT" FOR INPUT AS #1
Count=0
DO UNTIL EOF(1)
    LINE INPUT #1, Aname$
    Count=Count+1
LOOP
CLOSE #1
DIM Aname$(Count)
OPEN "A:\QBasic\LIST.DAT" FOR INPUT AS #1
FOR I=1 TO Count: LINE INPUT #1, Aname$(I): NEXT I
CLOSE #1
FOR I=1 TO Count: PRINT Aname$(I): NEXT I
END
```

However, the disadvantage of having to read a long file to find out the total number of records before it could be read into an array to, say, be sorted is only too obvious.

The general disadvantage in using sequential data files is that there is no way in which we could know the precise position, within the file, of a given record. This means that, if we wanted to find a given record, we must read in turn each record of the file from its beginning.

Problem 6.2

Convert the solution to Problem 6.1 to incorporate the SEQUENAP program as a procedure so that you can create, retrieve and append to a sequential file.

Then convert the PROCSORT program (to be found in section 'Passing Arrays to Procedures' in Chapter 5) so that retrieved data can be sorted in alphabetical order. Use the data file LIST to verify that all the options offered by your program perform as expected.

Save the resulting program under the filename SEQFILE.

Random Access Files

Random-access data files are like a collection of equal-length sequential files, which means that each file can have a number of records (each with a record length specified by parameter LENgth). A visual representation of random access data files is shown below:

```
                   1         2         3         4
1234567890123456789012345678901234567890123456789012345678901234
--------------------------------------------
ADAMS M.            02-1893   iissssdddddddd
SMITH A. D.         03-864243 iissssdddddddd
LONGFELLOW A. B. C. 01-5513567iissssdddddddd
--------------------------------------------
```

Each row represents a record and each record is divided into 6 'fields'. The first field, which is 20 characters long, contains names, the second, which is 10 characters long, contains phone numbers, the third to the fifth field contains numerical data which is encoded to strings of lengths 2, 4 and 8 characters, representing integer, single- and double-precision floating-point numbers, respectively. Thus the record length of each row in the above representation 48 characters (20+10+2+4+8 = 44).

QuickBASIC can store data in random access files by using either of two formats; by storing all data as strings which requires you to define a record by the FIELD statement, or by storing composite data which requires you to define a record by the TYPE..END TYPE statement. Both definitions will be discussed.

In the former case, numeric values must be converted to strings before they can be stored. To do this, QuickBASIC provides four functions, namely MKI$, MKL$, MKS$, and MKD$ which 'make' integers, long integers, single- and double-precision floating-point numbers into strings of 2, 4, 4, and 8 characters long. Functions CVI, CVL, CVS, and CVD 'convert' these strings back to numbers, so they can be used in expressions. In the latter case, you don't need to so convert data, but the penalty is that all records must remain the same size, irrespective of the actual information held in them. An example of the flexibility available with the former case of storing records is given in Appendix C.

Defining Records by FIELD

The length of a record is declared in the OPEN statement, by assigning it to variable LEN, as follows:

```
OPEN <filename> AS #n LEN = L
```

The statement permits writing, reading, adding or changing a record of a random file.

The precise composition of each record is declared in the FIELD statement by including the length of each field and its string variable name. For the record structure of the file discussed above, this would take the form:

```
FIELD #n 20 AS Fcust$, 10 AS Ftel$, 2 AS Funits$, 4 AS Fprice$,
        8 AS Ftotal$
```

where Fcust$ is the field name of a customer and is 20 characters long, Ftel$ is the customer's telephone number and is 10 characters long, Funits$ represents the number of phone units used by the customer (integer, encrypted as 2 characters), Funival$ and Ftotal$ represent the unit value and the total amount due (single- and double- precision floating-point numbers, encrypted as 4 and 8 characters respectively).

Note that field names have been preceded by the letter F to easily distinguish them from other program variables. The reason for this has to do with the way QuickBASIC assigns the contents of a string variable to a field string. The assignment is made with the use of the LSET statement, as follows:

```
LSET Fcust$=Aname$
```

assigning to Fcust$ a string of w (in our case, 20) characters long. If Aname$ is longer than w characters, then only the leftmost w characters will be assigned. If it is less than w characters, then it left justifies the string and adds the appropriate number of spaces.

Never assign a value to a field variable by using LET. You *must* use LSET and for this reason we use an F as the first letter of a field variable so mistakes can be avoided.

Random access files are inefficient users of file space. For example, the first record above contains a short name, yet a standard length is set aside for each field. On the other hand, information can be found easily. The third record, for example, begins at character number 3*LEN, where LEN is the length of the record. LEN can be any number from 1 to 32767, but if it is not specified in the OPEN statement it defaults to 128.

Creating and Retrieving Random Files:
Data can be stored in a random file with the use of the

```
PUT #n, r
```

command, which places data into record r. Numeric data must have been made to strings with the use of the MKI$, MKL$, MKS$, or MKD$ functions. Assignments to field string variables must be made with the LSET statement.

Data can be read from a random file with the use of the

```
GET #n, r
```

command, which allows you to read record r. Field string variables can be assigned to program variables with the use of the LET statement. Numerically encrypted variables must be converted with the use of CVI, CVL, CVS or CVD functions.

Unlike sequential files, there is no need to close random files after recording information in them in order to read from them. You can simply use the GET command and specify the required record r. However, this record must exist in the file. As the total number of characters in a file can be found from the

```
LOF(n)
```

function, dividing the value of LOF function by LEN gives the number of records in a random file.

The program on the next page will help to illustrate how random access files can be created using the INPUT LINE statement. Save it under the filename RANCREAT (which stands for RANdom CREATe).

```
REM CREATE A RANDOM DATA FILE
READ New
DIM Aname$(New), Phone$(New), Units%(New), Price(New),
      Amount#(New)
FOR I=1 TO New
    READ Aname$(I), Phone$(I), Units%(I), Price(I)
    Amount#(I)=Units%(I)*Price(I)
NEXT I
INPUT "NAME TO SAVE UNDER? ", Filename$
OPEN Filename$ AS #1 LEN = 44
FIELD #1, 20 AS Fcust$, 10 AS Ftel$, 2 AS Funits$, 4 AS Funival$,
          8 AS Ftotal$
FOR I=1 TO New
    LSET Fcust$=Aname$(I)
    LSET Ftel$=Phone$(I)
    LSET Funits$=MKI$(Units%(I))
    LSET Funival$=MKS$(Price(I))
    LSET Ftotal$=MKD$(Amount#(I))
    PUT #1, I
NEXT I
CLOSE #1
DATA 3
DATA "ADAMS M.", "02-1893", 350, 8
DATA "SMITH A. D.", "03-864243", 380, 8
DATA "LONGFELLOW A. B. C.", "01-5513567", 415, 8
END
```

The following program will retrieve a specified random access file provided it was created by the same FIELD format and has the same record length. Type it into your computer and **S**ave it under the filename RANRETR (RANdom RETRieve). Then use the RANCREAT program to create a random file (call it RANDATA) and the RANRETR program to retrieve it.

```
REM RETRIEVE A RANDOM DATA FILE
INPUT "FILE NAME TO LOAD? ", Filename$
OPEN Filename$ AS #2 LEN = 44
FIELD #2, 20 AS Fcust$, 10 AS Ftel$, 2 AS Funits$, 4 AS Funival$,
          8 AS Ftotal$
Max=LOF(2)\44
DIM Aname$(Max), Phone$(Max), Units%(Max), Price(Max),
      Amount#(Max)
```

```
FOR I=1 TO Max
     GET #2, I
     LET Aname$(I)=Fcust$
     LET Phone$(I)=Ftel$
     LET Units%(I)=CVI(Funits$)
     LET Price(I)=CVS(Funival$)
     LET Amount#(I)=CVD(Ftotal$)
NEXT I
CLOSE #2
CLS
PRINT "Customer"; TAB(22); "Telephone"; TAB(35); "Units";
       TAB(43); "Price"; TAB(50); "Amount"
FOR I=1 TO Max
     PRINT Aname$(I); TAB(22); Phone$(I); TAB(35); Units%(I);
            TAB(43); Price(I); TAB(50); Amount#(I)
NEXT I
END
```

Append, Edit, or Delete Records in Random Files:
Appending records to an existing random file can be achieved easily enough by first finding out the maximum number of records in the file with the help of the LOF(n)\LEN expression and then using the PUT command to write information into the file starting at the maximum number of records plus one.

Editing a record requires you to know its numerical position in the file in order to start writing at that record position the edited information.

Deleting records again requires you to know the numerical position of the record in the file, so that a null string can be LSET to the first field variable. The retrieve program could then be rewritten to test for spaces in the first field, and if found not to display such a record.

Problem 6.3

Implement the above suggestions relating to methods for appending, editing and deleting records in random files and incorporate into it the create and retrieve programs, using the SELECT CASE statement to provide a menu of choices. Save the resultant program under the filename RANFILE.

The solution to this problem is vital if you are to understand how random files work. So, do try it for yourself before looking up the solution at the back of the book. When you do have a look at the solution provided, bear in mind that there are better methods of solving the same problem. For example, it would be better to store information relating to the length of each record, the number of fields and their lengths and types, as well as their field names, in an index file. In this way, one program could create, retrieve, edit, etc., many different random data files. For such a program, see Appendix C.

Defining Records by TYPE

Records can be defined by the use of the TYPE..END TYPE statement which allows the creation and storing of data in a composite format; mixing string and numeric types. As a result, functions such as MKI$, MKL$, MKS$, and MKD$ which 'make' integers, long integers, single- and double-precision floating-point numbers into strings, and the functions CVI, CVL, CVS, and CVD which 'convert' these strings back to their corresponding values, are not used.

The definition of TYPE..END TYPE is given below using the same variable names as those used in the RANCREAT program:

```
TYPE RECORD
    Aname AS STRING * 20
    Phone AS STRING * 10
    Units AS INTEGER
    Price AS SINGLE
    Amount AS DOUBLE
END TYPE
```

To open a file and specify its length, now requires the following statement:

```
OPEN Filename$ FOR RANDOM AS #1 LEN = 44
```

The program listed on the next page is the same program as the RANCREAT program developed earlier. You could either edit that program, or re-type the new version. In either case, **S**ave it under the filename RANCRTYP (which stands for RANdom CReate with TYPe).

```
REM CREATE A RANDOM DATA FILE WITH TYPE
TYPE RECORD
    Aname AS STRING * 20
    Phone AS STRING * 10
    Units AS INTEGER
    Price AS SINGLE
    Amount AS DOUBLE
END TYPE
READ New
DIM Table(New) AS RECORD
FOR I = 1 TO New
    READ Table(I).Aname, Table(I).Phone, Table(I).Units,
            Table(I).Price
    Table(I).Amount = Table(I).Units * Table(I).Price
NEXT I
INPUT "NAME TO SAVE UNDER? ", Filename$
OPEN Filename$ FOR RANDOM AS #1 LEN = 44
FOR I = 1 TO New
PUT #1, I, Table(I)
NEXT I
CLOSE #1
DATA 3
DATA "ADAMS M.", "02-1893", 350, 8
DATA "SMTH A. D.", "03-864243", 380, 8
DATA "LONGFELLOW A. B. C.", "01-5513567", 415, 8
END
```

Note the use of the structured variable

```
Table(I).Aname
```

which refers to the element 'Aname' of the Ith entry in the array 'Table()'.

The equivalent program to retrieve random files with the use of the TYPE..END TYPE definition is given below:

```
REM RETRIEVE A RANDOM DATA FILE USING TYPE
TYPE RECORD
    Aname AS STRING * 20
    Phone AS STRING * 10
    Units AS INTEGER
    Price AS SINGLE
    Amount AS DOUBLE
END TYPE
```

```
INPUT "FILE NAME TO LOAD? ", Filename$
OPEN Filename$ FOR RANDOM AS #2 LEN = 44
Max = LOF(2) \ 44
DIM Table(Max) AS RECORD
FOR I = 1 TO Max
    GET #2, I, Table(I)
NEXT I
CLOSE #2
CLS
PRINT "Customer"; TAB(22); "Telphone"; TAB(35); "Units"; TAB(43);
        "Price"; TAB(50); "Amount"
FOR I = 1 TO Max
    PRINT Table(I).Aname; TAB(22); Table(I).Phone; TAB(35);
            Table(I).Units; TAB(43); Table(I).Price; TAB(50);
            Table(I).Amount
NEXT I
END
```

As before, you could either edit the RANRETR program, or re-type the new version given above. In either case, **S**ave the resultant program under the filename RANRETYP (which stands for RANdom REtrieve with TYPe).

Binary Files

A binary file is the most rudimentary type of files which offer the greatest flexibility, but their use imposes considerable responsibility on the programmer as they do not have any structure. They are a sequence of characters without any delimiters or records. The characters simply occupy positions 0, 1, 2, and so on, within the file.

Just like random files, binary files have only one, all-purpose, OPEN statement, namely

```
OPEN <filename> FOR BINARY AS #n
```

which opens a channel of communication to the mentioned file. The file can be of any type, including files created outside the QuickBASIC environment.

When a binary file is OPENed, there is a 'current file position' pointer which points to position 0. The statement

```
SEEK #n, p
```

can change the current position of the pointer to position p.

Following the SEEK #n, p statement with a

```
PUT #n X$
```

starts writing the contents of X$ from the current position of the pointer onwards, eventually moving the position of pointer to the position that follows the last character written.

Similarly, the statement

```
GET #n, m, X$
```

starts reading at the current file position m characters and assigns them to variable X$, and then moves the current position pointer to a position following the last character read.

Other tasks, such as finding the current position of the file pointer, or the length of the file, can be found with the use of the LOC(n) and LOF(n) functions.

It is obvious from what has been said above, that you can OPEN any file as a binary file and you can read any part of it or, indeed, write to any part of it. But writing to such a file, it simply overwrites what was there in the first place, so unless you know precisely how the file is constructed you could end up destroying the information held in it.

Error Handling

The ON ERROR statement can be used to specify an error handling routine. The general form of the statement is:

ON ERROR GOTO *label*

where *label* identifies the first line of the error routine.

In the simple example below the error routine has been attached to the RANRETR program and it starts at the label 'Errortrap'. Once error handling has been turned on with the ON ERROR GOTO statement, errors cause a jump to the error handling routine, instead of displaying the error message and ending execution. To resume execution, once such a jump has occurred, you must use the RESUME statement. RESUME by itself causes execution to be resumed with the statement that caused the error, RESUME NEXT causes execution to resume with the statement following the one that caused the error, while RESUME *label* causes execution to resume at the specified *label*.

In the program below the error trapping routine can be activated by pressing <Enter> in response to "FILE NAME TO LOAD". In addition, the program assigns the length of an OPENed file to L&, and if its value is zero, then the message "File does not exist" is printed on the screen and the file is KILLed (deleted from disc) because with random files, if a file does not exist one is created, and if it does exist it is OPENed for reading or appending. KILLing files that don't exist avoids accumulating a lot of zero length files.

```
REM RETRIEVE A RANDOM DATA FILE WITH ERROR TRAPPING
ON ERROR GOTO Errortrap
Start:
INPUT "FILE NAME TO LOAD? ", Filename$
OPEN Filename$ AS #2 LEN = 44
L&=LOF(2)
IF L&=0 THEN
    CLOSE#2
    PRINT "File does not exist": KILL Filename$
    GOTO Start
END IF
FIELD #2, 20 AS Fcust$, 10 AS Ftel$, 2 AS Funits$, 4 AS Funival$,
           8 AS Ftotal$
Max=LOF(2)\44
DIM Aname$(Max), Phone$(Max), Units%(Max), Price(Max),
      Amount#(Max)
FOR I=1 TO Max
    GET #2, I
    LET Aname$(I)=Fcust$
    LET Phone$(I)=Ftel$
    LET Units%(I)=CVI(Funits$)
    LET Price(I)=CVS(Funival$)
    LET Amount#(I)=CVD(Ftotal$)
NEXT I
CLOSE #2: CLS
PRINT "Customer"; TAB(22); "Telephone"; TAB(35); "Units";
        TAB(43); "Price"; TAB(50); "Amount"
FOR I=1 TO Max
    PRINT Aname$(I); TAB(22); Phone$(I); TAB(35); Units%(I);
           TAB(43); Price(I); TAB(50); Amount#(I)
NEXT I
END
```

```
Errortrap:
    IF ERR=64 THEN
      PRINT "Error No. ";ERR;" - Bad Filename"
    END IF
RESUME Start
```

Problem 6.4

Implement the error handling routine in the RANRETYP (RANdom REtrieve with TYPe) program discussed earlier. Save the resultant program under the filename RANERTYP.

Exercises

1. A record is kept of the production of each of eight machines at a factory. At the end of each week, a data card is prepared for each machine which records machine number (from 1 to 8), number of items produced and number of running hours. The information on this cards is then typed into a computer, not necessarily in order of machine number, so that the program can create a file to store it.

   Write a program to accomplish this task. The retrieve part of the program should also (a) calculate the number of items produced on each machine per hour, (b) add up the total production, (c) calculate the total hours worked, and (d) calculate the average production per hour. The results should be printed as a list in order of machine number, under appropriate headings.

2. Add appropriate procedures to the program appearing in Appendix C, so that the resulting program can append, edit, and delete records, in addition to its present capability of creating and retrieving records.

7. APPENDICES

A – QuickBASIC Reserved Words

The following table lists QuickBASIC's reserved words which must not be used as variable names in a program.

ABS	ACCESS	ALIAS	AND	ANY	APPEND
AS	ASC	ATN	BASE	BEEP	BINARY
BLOAD	BSAVE	BYVAL	CALL	CALLS	CASE
CDBL	CDECL	CHAIN	CHDIR	CHR$	CINT
CIRCLE	CLEAR	CLNG	CLOSE	CLS	COLOR
COM	COMMAND$	COMMON	CONST	COS	CSNG
CSRLIN	CVD	CVDMBF	CVI	CVL	CVS
CVSMBF	DATA	DATE$	DECLARE	DEF	DEFDBL
DEFINT	DEFLNG	DEFSNG	DEFSTR	DIM	DO
DOUBLE	DRAW	ELSE	ELSIF	END	ENDIF
ENVIRON	ENVIRON$	EOF	EQV	ERASE	ERDEV
ERDEV$	ERL	ERR	ERROR	EXIT	EXP
FIELD	FILEATTR	FILES	FIX	FN	FOR
FRE	FREEFILE	FUNCTION	GET	GOSUB	HEX$
IF	IMP	INKEY$	INP	INPUT	INPUT$
INSTR	INT	INTEGER	IOCTL	IOCTL$	IS
KEY	KILL	LBOUND	LCASE$	LEFT$	LEN
LET	LINE	LIST	LOC	LOCAL	LOCATE
LOCK	LOF	LOG	LONG	LOOP	LPOS
LPRINT	LSET	LTRIM$	MID$	MKD$	MKDIR
MKDMBF$	MKI$	MKL$	MKS$	MKSMBF$	MOD
NAME	NEXT	NOT	OCT$	OFF	ON
OPEN	OPTION	OR	OUT	OUTPUT	PAINT
PALETTE	PCOPY	PEEK	PEN	PLAY	PMAP
POINT	POKE	POS	PRESET	PRINT	PSET
PUT	RANDOM	RANDOMIZE	READ	REDIM	REM
RESET	RESTORE	RESUME	RETURN	RIGHT$	RMDIR
RND	RSET	RTRIM$	RUN	SADD	SCREEN
SEEK	SEG	SELECT	SETMEM	SGN	SHARED
SHELL	SIGNAL	SIN	SINGLE	SLEEP	SOUND
SPACE$	SPC	SQR	STATIC	STEP	STICK
STOP	STR$	STRIG	STRING	STRING$	SUB
SWAP	SYSTEM	TAB	TAN	THEN	TIME$
TIMER	TO	TROFF	TRON	TYPE	UNBOUND
UCASE$	UNLOCK	UNTIL	USING	VAL	VARPTR
VARPTR$	VARSEG	VIEW	WAIT	WEND	WHILE
WIDTH	WINDOW	WRITE	XOR		

B – Error Messages

QuickBASIC displays two different types of error messages: run-time and compile-time. Run-time errors messages occur when a compiled program is executed and are the result of errors detected by the compiler, while compile-time errors are errors in syntax encountered by the compiler.

Run-time errors, including file-system errors, have error codes between 0 and 255 which are displayed together with a short message. They can be trapped by an error-handling routine to retain program control should an error occurs with the use of the ON ERROR statement. The error routine can then divert program control based on the type of error that occurred. File-system errors (such as 'disk full'), are particularly suited to an error-handling routine.

If run-time errors are not trapped by an error-handling routine, then the program will be aborted on encountering an error condition. Furthermore, if you are executing a compiled .EXE file of your program direct from DOS, the short error messages that accompany the error numbers are not included in the error display.

Compile-time error messages appear on the screen with a brief description. They are the result of errors of syntax caused by missing symbols, misspelled commands, etc. If the compiler does not understand something in the source program, it automatically places you in the editor with the cursor positioned at the <OK> option of the dialogue box and the line causing the error highlighted. Pressing <Enter> clears the error message, allowing you to edit the offending statement.

Run-Time Errors:

Run-time errors have error codes between 0 and 255, and have the following meaning:

Code	*Meaning*
3	A RETURN was detected without a matching GOSUB.
5	An attempt has been made to pass an inappropriate argument to a statement or function.

6 An overflow condition has occurred as a result of a calculation which has produced a value which is too large to be represented in the indicated numeric type.

7 The out-of-memory error can be caused by many situations, including dimensioning too large an array.

9 An attempt has been made to use an array subscript larger than the maximum value given in the DIMension statement.

11 An attempt has been made to divide by zero or to raise zero to a negative power.

14 The string storage space of 64 kbytes has been exceeded.

19 There is no RESUME statement in error-handling routine.

20 A RESUME statement has been executed without the occurrence of an error.

24 The specified device time-out value for a communication status line has expired.

25 A hardware device error has occurred.

27 The printer is out of paper or it may be turned off.

39 CASE ELSE expected.

40 Variable required.

50 Given the file's record length, an attempt has been made to define a set of field variables in a FIELD statement which are too long.

51 A malfunction has occurred within the QuickBASIC run-time system. Call the Technical Support Group.

52 The channel number you gave in a file statement is not the same as the one given in an OPEN statement, or the channel number may be out of the 1-15 range.

53 The specified filename could not be found on the logged/indicated drive.

54 An attempt has been made to use PUT/PUT$ or GET/GET$ on a sequential file.

55 An attempt has been made to open or delete an already opened file.

56 FIELD statement active.

57 A hardware device I/O error has occurred.

58 An attempt has been made to specify a new name argument in the NAME command which already exists.

59 Bad record length.

61 The logged disc is full.

62 An attempt has been made to read more data from a file than it had in it. The error can also be caused by trying to read from a sequential file opened for output or append.

63 A negative number or one larger than 16,777,215 was given as the record number to a random file.

64 Invalid characters have been used in naming a file in a FILES, KILL, or NAME statement.

67 An attempt has been made to create too many files in a drive's root directory or by using an invalid filename.

68 The device you have tried to OPEN does not exist.

69 An attempt has been made to INPUT characters into an already full communications buffer.

70 An attempt has been made to write to a write-protected disc.

71 The door of the floppy disc drive is open or there is no disc in it.

72 The disc controller adaptor indicates a hard media error in one or more sectors.

73 Advanced feature unavailable.

74 An attempt has been made to rename a file across discs or directories.

75 An inappropriate path/file access name has been used in a command, such as OPEN, RENAME, etc.

76 The path specified during a command, such as OPEN, etc., cannot be found.

C –
Creating & Retrieving General Random Data

The program below can create and retrieve any number of different random files. These can have any number of fields and any type of field specifications. For ease of understanding, the program is split into a short main program and several subprograms. The main program is listed below.

```
DECLARE SUB CREATE ()
DECLARE SUB RETRIEVE ()
DECLARE SUB MAKEIDX (Filename$, Reclen%)
DECLARE SUB READIDX (Filename$, Reclen%)
REM CREATE, RETRIEVE GENERAL RANDOM FILES
REM $DYNAMIC
DIM Fldlens%(1), Fldnames$(1), Fldtype$(1), Fldvar$(1)
CLS
DO
PRINT "1. Create a File"
PRINT "2. Retrieve File"
PRINT "0. Quit"
PRINT:INPUT "CHOOSE (0/1/2)"; Q
SELECT CASE Q
    CASE 1
     CALL CREATE
    CASE 2
     CALL RETRIEVE
    CASE ELSE
    PRINT "Finished"
    END
END SELECT
PRINT:PRINT "Done"
LOOP WHILE Q
```

The main program uses the CREATE and RETRIEVE subprograms to respectively create and retrieve a new database. For simplicity, the program does not contain any error trapping routines, therefore trying to retrieve a file that doesn't exist will flag an error. Subprogram CREATE is listed on the next page.

```
SUB CREATE
    SHARED Numflds%, Fldnames$(), Fldlens%(), Fldtype$(),
                Fldvar$()
    ERASE Fldlens%, Fldnames$, Fldtype$, Fldvar$
    INPUT "NAME TO SAVE UNDER? ", Filename$
    INPUT "Number of fields:", Numflds%
    DIM Fldlens%(Numflds%), Fldnames$(Numflds%)
    DIM Fldtype$(Numflds%), Fldvar$(Numflds%)
    FOR I=1 TO Numflds%
      PRINT "Heading for field "; I;: INPUT " ", Fldnames$(I)
      PRINT "Datatype of field "; I;: INPUT " ", Temp$
      Fldtype$(I)=UCASE$(Temp$)
      SELECT CASE Fldtype$(I)
        CASE "INTEGER"
          Fldlens%(I)=2: Fldtype$(I)="%"
        CASE "LONG"
          Fldlens%(I)=4: Fldtype$(I)="&"
        CASE "SINGLE"
          Fldlens%(I)=4: Fldtype$(I)="!"
        CASE "DOUBLE"
          Fldlens%(I)=8: Fldtype$(I)="#"
        CASE "STRING"
          PRINT "How many chars in "Fldnames$(I)":";
          INPUT "", Fldlens%(I): Fldtype$(I)="$"
      END SELECT
    NEXT I
    CALL MAKEIDX(Filename$, Reclen%)
    OPEN Filename$+".DAT" AS #1 LEN = Reclen%
    FIELD#1,Fldlens%(1) AS Fldvar$(1)
    Count%=Fldlens%(1)
    FOR I=2 TO Numflds%
      FIELD#1, Count% AS DUM$, Fldlens%(I) AS Fldvar$(I)
      Count%=Count%+Fldlens%(I)
    NEXT I: Recno%=0
    DO
      PRINT "<Enter> to add data <End> to quit"
      INPUT "", A$: IF UCASE$(A$)="END" THEN EXIT DO
      Recno%=Recno%+1
      FOR J=1 to Numflds%: PRINT Fldnames$(J)":";
        SELECT CASE Fldtype$(J)
          CASE "%"
            INPUT "",A%: LSET Fldvar$(J)=MKI$(A%)
```

```
        CASE "&"
         INPUT "",A&: LSET Fldvar$(J)=MKL$(A&)
        CASE "!"
         INPUT "",A!: LSET Fldvar$(J)=MKS$(A!)
        CASE "#"
         INPUT "",A#: LSET Fldvar$(J)=MKD$(A#)
        CASE "$"
         INPUT "",A$: LSET Fldvar$(J)=A$
      END SELECT
     NEXT J: PUT#1, Recno%
    LOOP: CLOSE #1
    PRINT USING "#### Records created in file &_.DAT";
          Recno%, Filename$
END SUB
```

The subprogram asks the user for a name under which to save your created database, then the number of fields Numflds% the new database is going to have. Following this, the program asks for the 'Heading' of each field, its type (that is whether it is Integer, Long, Single, Double or String) and appropriately assigns the correct number of bytes required to hold the numeric field types. If you specify that the field is a String, then you are asked for the length of the field in characters.

Once all the above information is entered, the program CALLs the MAKEIDX subprogram to make the .IDX file which contains the number of fields, their appropriate lengths and types. The subprogram calculates and returns the record length Reclen%. The MAKEIDX subprogram is listed below.

```
SUB MAKEIDX(Filename$, Reclen%)
    SHARED Numflds%, Fldlens%(), Fldtype$(), Fldnames$()
    DIM FLEN$(Numflds%), FTYPE$(Numflds%)
    DIM HEAD$(Numflds%)
    OPEN Filename$+".IDX" AS #1 LEN = 2+23*Numflds%
    FIELD #1, 2 AS FLDS$
    LSET FLDS$=MKI$(Numflds%)
    Reclen%=0
    FOR I=1 TO Numflds%
     FIELD#1, 3*I-1 AS DUM$, 2 AS FLEN$(I), 1 AS FTYPE$(I)
     FIELD#1, 3*Numflds%+20*I-18 AS DUM$, 20 AS HEAD$(I)
     LSET FLEN$(I)=MKI$(Fldlens%(I))
     LSET FTYPE$(I)=Fldtype$(I)
```

```
    LSET HEAD$(I)=Fldnames$(I)
    Reclen%=Reclen%+Fldlens%(I)
  NEXT I: PUT#1,1
  PRINT "File "Filename$".IDX created OK.": CLOSE#1
  ERASE FLEN$, FTYPE$, HEAD$
END SUB
```

The fourth line of the above subprogram OPENs a file with the given filename, but with extension .IDX, which has a length LEN = 2+23*Numflds%. This is equivalent to 2 bytes for the number of fields, plus 3*Numflds% for field definitions made up of 2 bytes to hold an integer number describing the length of each field, 1 byte to describe the type of field (integer as %, long integer as &, single-precision as !, double-precision as #, or string as $), and 20 bytes describing the headings of each field.

The following line creates the FIELD image with 2 bytes for the number of fields. The FIELD image is then built up with the first two statements within the FOR...NEXT loop.

In this first FIELD statement within the loop, namely

```
FIELD#1, 3*I-1 AS DUM$, 2 AS FLEN$(I), 1 AS FTYPE$(I)
```

the 3*I–1 is equivalent to 2+3*(I–1); 2 being the dummy for number of fields, while 3*(I–1) being the number of characters used up in the preceding fields, 2 for field length and 1 for type of field.

In this first FIELD statement within the loop, namely

```
FIELD#1, 3*Numflds%+20*I-18 AS DUM$, 20 AS HEAD$(I)
```

the 3*Numflds% is equivalent to 2*Numflds% for the lengths of the fields plus 1*Numflds% for the types of the fields, while 20*I–18 is equivalent to 2 for the number of fields (accounted for previously), plus 20*(I–1) dummy bytes for the length of the preceding fields.

The schematic diagram, shown on the next page, will help to explain how the FIELD is being built up in the .IDX file. The diagram is drawn assuming the number of fields Numflds% = 3.

On return from the MAKEIDX subprogram back to the CREATE subprogram, the .DAT file is OPENed with the correct record length (Reclen%) which was calculated within the MAKEIDX subprogram. The FIELD image of the file is then constructed in a similar manner to that of the .IDX file.

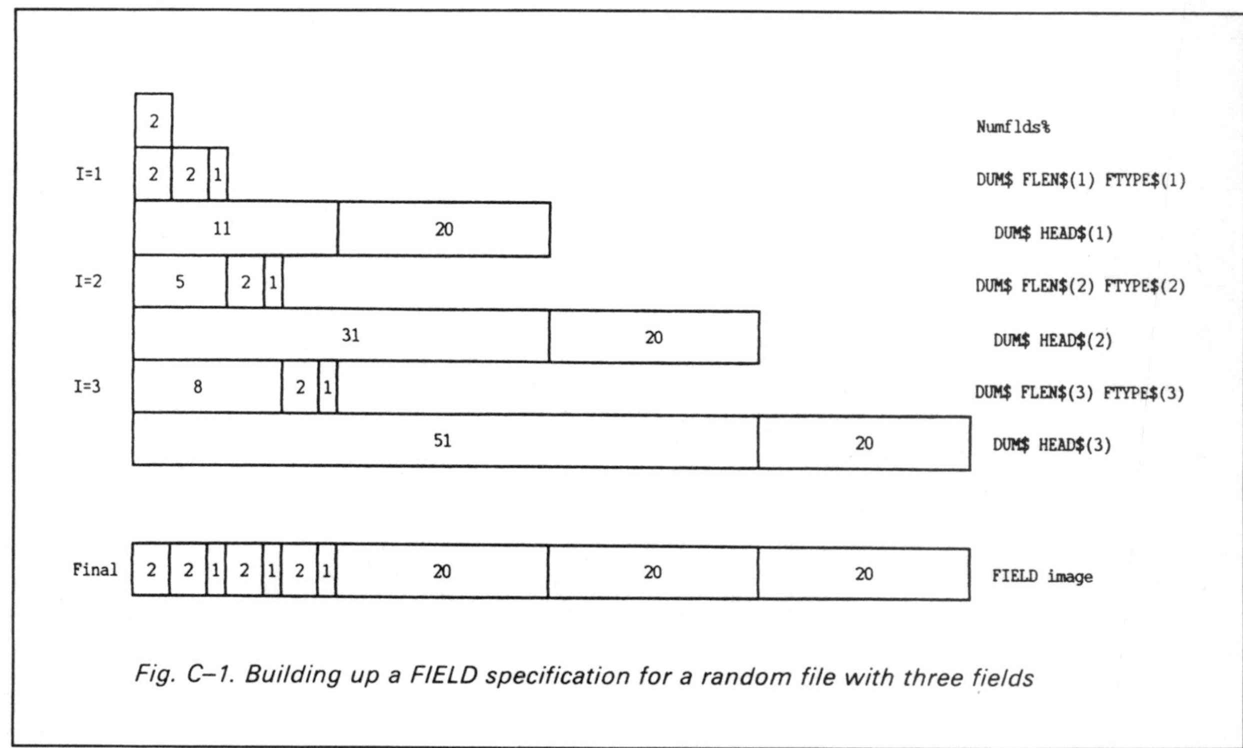

Fig. C–1. Building up a FIELD specification for a random file with three fields

The retrieve option of the main program makes use of the RETRIEVE subprogram which is listed below.

```
SUB RETRIEVE
    SHARED Numflds%, Fldlens%(), Fldtype$(), Fldnames$(),
            Fldvar$()
    INPUT "FILE NAME TO LOAD? ", Filename$
    CALL READIDX(Filename$, Reclen%)
    OPEN Filename$+".DAT" AS #1 LEN = Reclen%
    FIELD#1, Fldlens%(1) AS Fldvar$(1)
    Count%=Fldlens%(1)
    FOR I=2 TO Numflds%
     FIELD#1, Count% AS DUM$, Fldlens%(I) AS Fldvar$(I)
     Count%=Count%+Fldlens%(I)
    NEXT I
    Numrecs%=LOF(1)\Reclen%
    FOR I=1 TO Numrecs%
     GET#1, I
     FOR J=1 to Numflds%
      PRINT Fldnames$(J)":";
      SELECT CASE Fldtype$(J)
       CASE "%"
        A%=CVI(Fldvar$(J)): PRINT A%
       CASE "&"
        A&=CVL(Fldvar$(J)): PRINT A&
       CASE "!"
        A!=CVS(Fldvar$(J)): PRINT A!
       CASE "#"
        A#=CVD(Fldvar$(J)): PRINT A#
       CASE "$"
        A$=Fldvar$(J): PRINT A$
      END SELECT
     NEXT J
     PRINT:PRINT "Press any key to continue"
     A$=INPUT$(1)
    NEXT I: CLOSE #1
    PRINT USING "#### Records read from file &_.DAT";
           Numrecs%, Filename$
END SUB
```

The subprogram CALLs the READIDX subprogram which reads the .IDX file to find the structure of the file. READIDX is listed on the next page.

```
SUB READIDX(Filename$, Reclen%)
    SHARED Numflds%, Fldlens%(), Fldtype$(), Fldnames$(),
            Fldvar$()
    ERASE Fldlens%, Fldnames$, Fldtype$, Fldvar$
    OPEN Filename$+".IDX" AS #1 LEN = 2
    FIELD#1, 2 AS FLDS$: GET#1,1
    Numflds%=CVI(FLDS$): CLOSE#1
    DIM FLEN$(Numflds%), FTYPE$(Numflds%)
    DIM HEAD$(Numflds%)
    DIM Fldlens%(Numflds%), Fldnames$(Numflds%)
    DIM Fldtype$(Numflds%), Fldvar$(Numflds%)
    OPEN Filename$+".IDX" AS #1 LEN = 2+23*Numflds%
    FIELD #1, 2 AS FLDS$
    LSET FLDS$=MKI$(Numflds%)
    FOR I=1 TO Numflds%
     FIELD#1, 3*I-1 AS DUM$, 2 AS FLEN$(I), 1 AS FTYPE$(I)
     FIELD#1, 3*Numflds%+20*I-18 AS DUM$, 20 AS HEAD$(I)
    NEXT I: GET#1,1: Reclen%=0
    FOR I=1 TO Numflds%
     Fldlens%(I)=CVI(FLEN$(I))
     Fldtype$(I)=FTYPE$(I)
     Fldnames$(I)=HEAD$(I)
     Reclen%=Reclen%+Fldlens%(I)
    NEXT I
    PRINT "File "Filename$".IDX read OK.": CLOSE#1
    ERASE FLEN$, FTYPE$, HEAD$
END SUB
```

D -
Solutions to Problems

In the program listings presented in this section, it is sometimes necessary to break a long Basic line into two, or three, text lines because of the width limitations imposed by the book. The continuation line(s) of such code is indented by six spaces so that it is easily recognisable (as is the case with the first PRINT statement of the solution to Problem 2.2 below). However, when typing such program lines into the editor, make sure they are entered as one line only, otherwise an error will be generated by the compiler.

Problem 1.1

```
REM TEMPERATURE CONVERSION
INPUT "Enter Degrees F value ", F
C=(F-32)*5/9
PRINT SPC(1); F; " Degrees F ="; SPC(1); C; " Degrees C"
END
```

Problem 2.1

```
REM TIME CONVERSION
PRINT "DAYS", "HOURS", "MINUTES", "TOTAL MIN"
READ Days, Hours, Minutes
DATA 2, 10, 30
Total=Days*24*60+Hours*60+Minutes
PRINT Days; TAB(15); Hours; TAB(30); Minutes; TAB(45); Total
END
```

Problem 2.2

```
REM AVERAGES
INPUT "Enter three numbers ", A, B, C
Sum=A+B+C
Average=Sum/3
PRINT "VALUES:"; SPC(5); "A"; SPC(5); "B"; SPC(5); "C";
      SPC(5); "AVERAGE"
PRINT TAB(12); A; TAB(18); B; TAB(24); C; TAB(30); Average
END
```

Problem 3.1

```
REM SQUARE X
CLS: LOCATE 5,1
FOR I=1 TO 15
    PRINT TAB(34);
    FOR J=1 TO 15
      PRINT "X";
    NEXT J
    PRINT
NEXT I
END
```

Problem 3.2

```
REM COMPOUND INTEREST
DEFINT N,Years
INPUT "Enter original money lent ", Original
INPUT "Enter interest rate ", Rate
INPUT "Enter No. of years ", Years
PRINT SPC(1); "YEAR"; SPC(12); "AMOUNT"
FOR N=1 TO Years
    Amount=Original*(1+Rate/100)^N
    Form$="#####    ####,###.##"
    PRINT USING Form$; N, Amount
NEXT N
END
```

Problem 3.3

```
REM THREE NUMBER SORT
DO
    INPUT "Enter three numbers " ,A, B, C
    IF A = -1 THEN END
    WHILE A < B OR B < C
     IF A < B THEN
      Temp=A
      A=B
      B=Temp
     END IF
     IF B < C THEN
      Temp=B
      B=C
      C=Temp
     END IF
    WEND
    PRINT A, B, C
LOOP UNTIL False
END
```

Problem 3.4

```
REM IMPERIAL TO MKS CONVERSION
READ A, B, C
DATA 4.54609, 0.3048, 0.453592
DO:PRINT
    INPUT "GALLONS/FEET/POUNDS/QUIT (1/2/3/4) "; X: PRINT
    SELECT CASE X
     CASE 1
      INPUT "ENTER NR OF GALLONS ", Gallons
      Litres=A*Gallons
      PRINT Gallons; " GALLONS = "; Litres; " LITRES"
     CASE 2
      INPUT "ENTER NR OF FEET ", Feet
      Metres=B*Feet
      PRINT Feet; " FEET = "; Metres; " METRES"
     CASE 3
      INPUT "ENTER NR OF POUNDS ", Pounds
      Kilos=C*Pounds
      PRINT Pounds; " POUNDS = "; Kilos; " KILOS"
     CASE 4
      PRINT "Finished"
      END
     CASE ELSE
     PRINT "Wrong range ... Try again"
    END SELECT
LOOP UNTIL False
```

Problem 4.1

```
REM STOCKTAKING
DIM Item$(4)
FOR I=1 TO 4: READ Item$(I): NEXT I
DO: PRINT
     INPUT "WHICH ITEM "; Xname$
     IF UCASE$(Xname$)="END" THEN END
     FOR I=1 TO 4
       IF UCASE$(Xname$)=LEFT$(Item$(I),3) THEN
         PRINT ">>>>>> "; LEFT$(Item$(I),16); " ";
                  MID$(Item$(I),18,3); " IN STOCK AT £";
                  RIGHT$(Item$(I),4); " EACH"
       END IF
     NEXT I
LOOP UNTIL False
DATA "INK ERASER           ,200,0.10"
DATA "PENCIL ERASER        ,320,0.15"
DATA "TYPING ERASER        ,25  ,0.25"
DATA "CORRECTION FLUID ,150,0.50"
```

Problem 4.2

```
REM FIBONACCI SERIES
INPUT "HOW MANY TERMS "; N
DIM A(N),B(N-1): A(1)=1: A(2)=1
FOR I=3 TO N
     A(I)=A(I-2)+A(I-1)
NEXT I:REM ALL TERMS STORED IN A()
FOR I=1 TO N-1
     B(I)=(A(I)+A(I+1))/2
NEXT I: REM AVERAGES STORED IN B()
PRINT "F. SERIES"; SPC(10); "AVERAGES"
FOR I=1 TO N: PRINT USING "  ###"; A(I);
     IF I<>N THEN
       PRINT USING "        ###,###.##"; B(I)
     END IF
NEXT I: PRINT
END
```

Problem 4.3

```
REM SPECIFY NUMBER/LETTER TO PRINT LETTER/NUMBER
DO
    PRINT "1. SPECIFY NUMBER TO PRINT LETTER"
    PRINT "2. SPECIFY LETTER TO PRINT NUMBER"
    PRINT "3. END PROGRAM"
    DO:PRINT: INPUT "Choose (1/2/3) ", Which
    LOOP UNTIL Which >0 AND Which <4
    SELECT CASE Which
     CASE 1
      DO
       INPUT "Enter number 1 - 26 ", Number
      LOOP UNTIL Number>0 AND Number<27
      PRINT CHR$(64+Number): PRINT
     CASE 2
      DO
       INPUT "Enter a letter ", Letter$
      LOOP UNTIL ASC(Letter$)>63 AND ASC(Letter$)<91
      PRINT ASC(Letter$)–64: PRINT
     CASE 3
      END
    END SELECT
LOOP UNTIL False
```

Problem 4.4

```
REM BUBBLE SORT
READ N: DIM Employee$(N)
FOR I=1 TO N: READ Employee$(I): NEXT I
DO
    INPUT "OUTPUT TO SCREEN OR PRINTER? (S/P) ", Q$
LOOP UNTIL UCASE$(Q$)="S" OR UCASE$(Q$)="P"
IF UCASE$(LEFT$(Q$,1))="P" THEN
    FOR I=1 TO N: LPRINT Employee$(I): NEXT I
ELSE
    FOR I=1 TO N: PRINT Employee$(I): NEXT I
END IF
IF UCASE$(LEFT$(Q$,1))="P" THEN
    LPRINT: LPRINT: LPRINT "SORTED INFORMATION"
ELSE
    PRINT: PRINT: PRINT "SORTED INFORMATION"
END IF:M=N
FOR J=1 TO N-1
    M=M-1: Flag=0
    FOR I=1 TO M
     IF Employee$(I)>Employee$(I+1) THEN
      Flag=1
      Temp$=Employee$(I+1)
      Employee$(I+1)=Employee$(I)
      Employee$(I)=Temp$
     END IF
    NEXT I
    IF UCASE$(LEFT$(Q$,1))="P" THEN
     LPRINT: LPRINT J
     FOR I=1 TO N: LPRINT Employee$(I): NEXT I
    ELSE
     PRINT: PRINT J
     FOR I=1 TO N: PRINT Employee$(I): NEXT I
    END IF
    A$=INPUT$(1): IF Flag=0 THEN END
NEXT J
DATA 5
DATA "WILSON M.  ,ROOM 1.24, 395"
DATA "SMITH M.   ,ROOM 2.6  , 7315"
DATA "JONES B.M. ,ROOM 6.19, 1698"
DATA "SMITH A.A. ,ROOM 2.12, 456"
DATA "BROWN C.   ,ROOM 3.1  , 432"
```

Problem 5.1

```
REM NEWTON'S METHOD OF FINDING SQUARE ROOTS
INPUT "Enter a number ", Xvalue
INPUT "Guess a value ", Guess
FOR I=1 TO 30
     Ratio=Xvalue/Guess
     Average=(Ratio+Guess)/2.0
     IF ABS(Ratio-Guess) < 0.001 THEN
       PRINT "Square root of "; Xvalue; " = "; Average
       PRINT "Found in "; I; " Iterations"
       END
     END IF
     Guess=Average
NEXT I
PRINT "NOT CONVERGING IN "; I-1; " ITERATIONS"
END
```

Problem 5.2

```
DECLARE FUNCTION Volume!(R!, H!)
DECLARE FUNCTION Round!(X!, D%)
REM VOLUME OF A CYLINDER
INPUT "RADIUS OF CYLINDER "; Radius
INPUT "HEIGHT OF CYLINDER "; Height
PRINT "VOLUME="; Volume(Radius, Height)
END
FUNCTION Volume (R, H)
     Pi=3.141592654
     Barea=Pi*R^2
     Number=Barea*H
     Volume=Round(Number, 2)
END FUNCTION
FUNCTION Round(X, D%)
     Round=INT(X*10^D%+0.5)/10^D%
END DEF
```

Problem 5.3

```
DECLARE SUB Volume (R!, H!, Result!)
DECLARE FUNCTION Round! (X!, D%)
REM VOLUME OF A CYLINDER
INPUT "RADIUS OF CYLINDER "; Radius
INPUT "HEIGHT OF CYLINDER "; Height
CALL Volume(Radius, Height, Result)
PRINT "VOLUME="; Result
END
SUB Volume (R, H, Res)
    Pi = 3.141592654#
    Barea = Pi * R ^ 2
    Number = Barea * H
    Res = Round(Number, 2)
END SUB
FUNCTION Round (X, D%)
    Round = INT(X * 10 ^ D% + .5) / 10 ^ D%
END FUNCTION
```

Problem 6.1

```
DECLARE SUB CREATES ()
DECLARE SUB RETRIEVES ()
REM PROGRAM TO CREATE & RETRIEVE SEQ. DATA
PRINT "1. Create"
PRINT "2. Retrieve"
PRINT:INPUT "CHOOSE (1/2)"; Q
SELECT CASE Q
    CASE 1
     CALL CREATES
    CASE 2
     CALL RETRIEVES
    CASE ELSE
     PRINT "Finished":END
END SELECT
SUB CREATES
    INPUT "NUMBER OF NEW ENTRIES? ", New
    DIM Aname$(New): I=0
    DO
     I=I+1: PRINT "";I;">";: LINE INPUT "", Aname$(I)
    LOOP UNTIL I=New OR Aname$(I)=""
    IF Aname$(I)="" THEN New=I-1
    INPUT "NAME TO SAVE UNDER? ", Filename$
    OPEN Filename$+".IDX" FOR OUTPUT AS #1
    WRITE #1, New: CLOSE #1
    OPEN Filename$+".DAT" FOR OUTPUT AS #2
    FOR I=1 TO New: PRINT #2, Aname$(I): NEXT I: CLOSE #2
END SUB
SUB RETRIEVES
    INPUT "FILE NAME TO LOAD? ", Filename$
    OPEN Filename$+".IDX" FOR INPUT AS #3
    INPUT #3, Total: DIM Aname$(Total): CLOSE #3
    OPEN Filename$+".DAT" FOR INPUT AS #4
    FOR I=1 TO Total: LINE INPUT #4, Aname$(I): NEXT I
    CLOSE #4
    FOR I=1 TO Total: PRINT Aname$(I): NEXT I
END SUB
```

Problem 6.2

```
DECLARE SUB CREATES ()
DECLARE SUB RETRIEVES ()
DECLARE SUB APPENDS ()
DECLARE SUB WHICHFILE (Filename$)
DECLARE SUB PROCSORT (Employee$(), N!)
REM PROGRAM TO CREATE, RETRIEVE & APPEND SEQ. DATA
CLS:PRINT "1. Create": PRINT "2. Retrieve"
PRINT "3. Append": PRINT "0. QUIT"
PRINT:INPUT "CHOOSE (0/1/2/3)"; Q
SELECT CASE Q
    CASE 1
     CALL CREATES
    CASE 2
     CALL RETRIEVES
    CASE 3
     CALL APPENDS
    CASE ELSE
     PRINT "Finished"
END SELECT
PRINT:PRINT "Done": END
SUB CREATES
    INPUT "NUMBER OF NEW ENTRIES? ", New
    DIM Aname$(New): I=0
    DO
     I=I+1: PRINT ""; I; ">";: LINE INPUT "", Aname$(I)
    LOOP UNTIL I=New OR Aname$(I)=""
    IF Aname$(I)="" THEN New=I-1
    PRINT "SAVE TO ";:
    CALL WHICHFILE(Filename$)
    OPEN Filename$+".IDX" FOR OUTPUT AS #1
    WRITE #1, New: CLOSE #1
    OPEN Filename$+".DAT" FOR OUTPUT AS #2
    FOR I=1 TO New: PRINT #2, Aname$(I): NEXT I: CLOSE #2
END SUB
SUB RETRIEVES
    PRINT "LOAD ";:
    CALL WHICHFILE(Filename$)
    OPEN Filename$+".IDX" FOR INPUT AS #3
    INPUT #3, Total: DIM Aname$(Total): CLOSE #3
    OPEN Filename$+".DAT" FOR INPUT AS #4
    FOR I=1 TO Total: LINE INPUT #4, Aname$(I): NEXT I
```

```
    CLOSE #4
    FOR I=1 TO Total: PRINT Aname$(I): NEXT I
    CALL PROCSORT(Aname$(), Total)
    PRINT:PRINT "SORTED DATA"
    FOR I=1 TO Total: PRINT Aname$(I): NEXT I
END SUB
SUB APPENDS
    PRINT "APPEND TO ";:
    CALL WHICHFILE(Filename$)
    OPEN Filename$+".IDX" FOR INPUT AS #1
    INPUT #1, Old: PRINT "NUMBER OF RECORDS = "; Old
    CLOSE #1
    INPUT "NUMBER OF NEW ENTRIES? ", New
    DIM Aname$(New): I=0
    DO
    I=I+1
    PRINT ""; I+Old; ">";: LINE INPUT "", Aname$(I)
    LOOP UNTIL I=New OR Aname$(I)=""
    IF Aname$(I)="" THEN New=I-1
    Total=Old+New
    OPEN Filename$+".DAT" FOR APPEND AS #2
    FOR I=1 TO New: PRINT #2, Aname$(I): NEXT I
    CLOSE #2
    OPEN Filename$+".IDX" FOR OUTPUT AS #1
    WRITE #1, Total
    CLOSE #1
END SUB
SUB WHICHFILE(Filename$)
    DO
     INPUT "WHICH FILE? ", Filename$
     IF Filename$="" THEN
       CLS
       SHELL "DIR A:\QBasic /W"
     END IF
    LOOP UNTIL Filename$<>""
    CLS
END SUB
```

```
SUB PROCSORT(Employee$(1),N)
    M=N
    FOR J=1 TO N-1
     M=M-1: Flag=0
     FOR I=1 TO M
      IF Employee$(I)>Employee$(I+1) THEN
       SWAP Employee$(I+1), Employee$(I)
       Flag=1
      END IF
     NEXT I
     IF Flag=0 THEN EXIT FOR
    NEXT J
END SUB
```

Problem 6.3

```
DECLARE SUB CREATERAN ()
DECLARE SUB RETRIEVRAN ()
DECLARE SUB APPENDRAN ()
DECLARE SUB EDITRAN ()
DECLARE SUB DELETERAN ()
REM CREATE, RETRIEVE, APPEND & EDIT RANDOM FILES
CLS:PRINT "1. Create a File": PRINT "2. Retrieve File"
PRINT "3. Append to File": PRINT "4. Edit a Record"
PRINT "5. Delete a Record": PRINT "0. Quit"
PRINT:INPUT "CHOOSE (0/1/2/3/4/5)"; Q
SELECT CASE Q
     CASE 1
      CALL CREATERAN
     CASE 2
      CALL RETRIEVERAN
     CASE 3
      CALL APPENDRAN
     CASE 4
      CALL EDITRAN
     CASE 5
      CALL DELETERAN
     CASE ELSE
      PRINT "Finished"
END SELECT
PRINT:PRINT "Done": END
DATA 3
DATA "ADAMS M.", "02-1893", 350, 8
DATA "SMTH A. D.", "03-864243" ,380, 8
DATA "LONGFELLOW A. B. C.", "01-5513567", 415, 8
SUB CREATERAN
     READ New
     DIM Aname$(New), Phone$(New), Units%(New)
     DIM Price(New), Amount#(New)
     FOR I=1 TO New
      READ Aname$(I), Phone$(I), Units%(I), Price(I)
      Amount#(I)=Units%(I)*Price(I)
     NEXT I
     INPUT "NAME TO SAVE UNDER? ", Filename$
     OPEN Filename$ AS #1 LEN = 44
     FIELD #1, 20 AS Fcust$, 10 AS Ftel$, 2 AS Funits$,
               4 AS Funival$, 8 AS Ftotal$
```

```
    FOR I=1 TO New
      LSET Fcust$=Aname$(I)
      LSET Ftel$=Phone$(I)
      LSET Funits$=MKI$(Units%(I))
      LSET Funival$=MKS$(Price(I))
      LSET Ftotal$=MKD$(Amount#(I)): PUT #1, I
    NEXT I: CLOSE #1
END SUB
SUB RETRIEVERAN
    INPUT "FILE NAME TO LOAD? ", Filename$
    OPEN Filename$ AS #2 LEN = 44
    FIELD #2, 20 AS Fcust$, 10 AS Ftel$, 2 AS Funits$,
              4 AS Funival$, 8 AS Ftotal$
    Max=LOF(2)\44
    DIM Aname$(Max), Phone$(Max), Units%(Max)
    DIM Price(Max), Amount#(Max)
    FOR I=1 TO Max
      GET #2, I
      LET Aname$(I)=Fcust$
      LET Phone$(I)=Ftel$
      LET Units%(I)=CVI(Funits$)
      LET Price(I)=CVS(Funival$)
      LET Amount#(I)=CVD(Ftotal$)
    NEXT I: CLOSE #2: CLS
    PRINT "Rec "; TAB(6); "Customer"; TAB(28); "Telphone";
            TAB(41); "Units"; TAB(49); "Price"; TAB(56); "Amount"
    FOR I=1 TO Max
      PRINT I; TAB(6);:
      IF LEFT$(Aname$(I),1)=" " THEN
        PRINT
      ELSE
        PRINT Aname$(I); TAB(28); Phone$(I); TAB(41);
              Units%(I); TAB(49); Price(I); TAB(56); Amount#(I)
      END IF
    NEXT I
END SUB
SUB APPENDRAN
    INPUT "FILE NAME TO APPEND TO? ", Filename$
    OPEN Filename$ AS #3 LEN = 44
    FIELD #3, 20 AS Fcust$, 10 AS Ftel$, 2 AS Funits$,
              4 AS Funival$, 8 AS Ftotal$
    Old=LOF(3)\44:PRINT "NUMBER OF RECORDS = "; Old
    INPUT "NUMBER OF NEW ENTRIES? ", New
```

```
    DIM Aname$(New), Phone$(New), Units%(New)
    DIM Price(New), Amount#(New): I=0
    DO
     I=I+1: PRINT ""; I+Old; ">";:
     INPUT ""; Aname$(I), Phone$(I), Units%(I), Price(I)
     Amount#(I)=Units%(I)*Price(I)
    LOOP UNTIL I=New OR Aname$(I)=""
    IF Aname$(I)="" THEN New=I-1
    FOR I=1 TO New
     LSET Fcust$=Aname$(I)
     LSET Ftel$=Phone$(I)
     LSET Funits$=MKI$(Units%(I))
     LSET Funival$=MKS$(Price(I))
     LSET Ftotal$=MKD$(Amount#(I)): PUT #3, I+Old
    NEXT I: CLOSE #3
END SUB
SUB EDITRAN
    INPUT "FILE NAME TO EDIT? ", Filename$
    OPEN Filename$ AS #4 LEN = 44
    FIELD #4, 20 AS Fcust$, 10 AS Ftel$, 2 AS Funits$,
              4 AS Funival$, 8 AS Ftotal$
    Old=LOF(4)\44:PRINT "NUMBER OF RECORDS = "; Old
    DO
     INPUT "RECORD TO EDIT? ", Rec
    LOOP UNTIL Rec<=Old
    CLS: PRINT "Customer"; TAB(22); "Telphone"; TAB(35);
               "Units"; TAB(43); "Price"; TAB(50); "Amount"
    GET #4, Rec
    PRINT Fcust$; TAB(22); Ftel$; TAB(35); CVI(Funits$);
          TAB(43); CVS(Funival$); TAB(50); CVD(Ftotal$)
    PRINT "EDIT TO": PRINT ""; Rec; ">";:
    INPUT ""; Aname$, Phone$, Units%, Price
    Amount#=Units%*Price
    LSET Fcust$=Aname$
    LSET Ftel$=Phone$
    LSET Funits$=MKI$(Units%)
    LSET Funival$=MKS$(Price)
    LSET Ftotal$=MKD$(Amount#)
    PUT #4, Rec
END SUB
```

```
SUB DELETERAN
    INPUT "FILE NAME TO CHANGE? ", Filename$
    OPEN Filename$ AS #5 LEN = 44
    FIELD #5, 20 AS Fcust$, 10 AS Ftel$, 2 AS Funits$,
              4 AS Funival$, 8 AS Ftotal$
    Old=LOF(5)\44: PRINT "NUMBER OF RECORDS = "; Old
    DO
     INPUT "RECORD TO DELETE? ", Rec
    LOOP UNTIL Rec<=Old
    CLS
    PRINT "Customer"; TAB(22); "Telphone"; TAB(35);
           "Units"; TAB(43); "Price"; TAB(50); "Amount"
    GET #5, Rec
    PRINT Fcust$; TAB(22); Ftel$; TAB(35); CVI(Funits$);
           TAB(43); CVS(Funival$); TAB(50); CVD(Ftotal$)
    INPUT "DELETE THIS RECORD? (Y/N) ", Q$
    IF UCASE$(LEFT$(Q$,1))="Y" THEN
     Aname$=""
     LSET Fcust$=Aname$
     PUT #5, Rec
    ELSE
    END IF
    CLOSE #5
END SUB
```

Problem 6.4

```
REM RETRIEVE A RANDOM DATA FILE USING TYPE
REM WITH ERROR TRAPPING
TYPE RECORD
      Aname AS STRING * 20
      Phone AS STRING * 10
      Units AS INTEGER
      Price AS SINGLE
      Amount AS DOUBLE
END TYPE
CLS
ON ERROR GOTO Errortrap
 Start:
      INPUT "FILE NAME TO LOAD? ", Filename$
      OPEN Filename$ FOR RANDOM AS #2 LEN = 44
      L& = LOF(2)
      IF L& = 0 THEN
        CLOSE #2
        PRINT "File does not exist": KILL Filename$
        GOTO Start
      END IF
      Max = LOF(2) \ 44
      DIM Table(Max) AS RECORD
      FOR I = 1 TO Max
        GET #2, I, Table(I)
      NEXT I
      CLOSE #2
      CLS
      PRINT "Customer"; TAB(22); "Telphone"; TAB(35); "Units";
                TAB(43); "Price"; TAB(50); "Amount"
      FOR I = 1 TO Max
        PRINT Table(I).Aname; TAB(22); Table(I).Phone; TAB(35);
                Table(I).Units; TAB(43); Table(I).Price; TAB(50);
                Table(I).Amount
      NEXT I
END
Errortrap:
      IF ERR = 64 THEN
        PRINT "Error No. "; ERR; " - Bad Filename"
      END IF
      RESUME Start
END
```

INDEX